THE GREAT COMPROMISE

How Catholics
and Protestants
are undoing
the Reformation
and fulfilling
prophecy

CLIFFORD GOLDSTEIN

Pacific Press® Publishing Association
Nampa, Idaho
Oshawa, Ontario, Canada

Edited by B. Russell Holt
Designed by Tim Larson
Cover photo by H. Horenstein © Photonica

Pacific Press® Publishing Association
Printed in the United States of America

ISBN 0-8163-1821-2

00 01 02 03 04 • 5 4 3 2 1

Contents

CHAPTER ONE

Scratched by Schrödinger's Cat

One of the most famous experiments in scientific history involved a cat.

Schrödinger's cat.

The feline was placed in a sealed box with some radioactive material, a device for detecting radioactive decay, poison gas safely stashed in a glass container, and a hammer poised over the glass. The detector was switched on long enough to create a 50/50 chance that one atom in the radioactive material would decay. If so, the detector would record the decay, causing the hammer to smash the glass, which would release the gas and kill the cat. If the atom didn't decay, the detector would not trigger the hammer, the poison would remain in the container, and Schrödinger's cat would live to see another day.

Because radioactive decay occurs at the quantum level—the level of individual atoms, photons, and sub-atomic entities, where events are purely random and predictable only in a statistical sense—no way existed to know, for sure, what happened to the cat except by opening the box. The scientist would have to look inside; only then could he know the feline's fate.

According to quantum physics, however, things aren't that simple. Quantum physics (or at least one interpretation of it) suggests that until the box is opened and a person looks inside, the cat exists in a "superposition of states,"[1] a sort of limbo in which the cat is neither dead or alive. Not until someone actually views the cat does it become one or the other, that is, dead or alive. According to this theory, the very act of looking changes reality and creates either a live cat (if the atom didn't decay) or a dead one (if the atom did). Either way, the fate of the cat isn't actually determined until someone looks at it.

"Quantum theory," wrote mathematical physicist Paul Davies, "requires that the system develops into a ghost-like hybrid state of live-dead cat until an observation is made, when *either* a live or dead cat will be perceived."[2]

This idea is, of course, ridiculous. Looking at the cat isn't going to change it. The cat is either dead or alive *before* the box is opened. Observation reveals only what's already there; it doesn't alter it. The whole point of the experiment with Schrödinger's cat was, in fact, to express the absurdity of this concept (known as the Copenhagen Interpretation) regarding what happens in the quantum realm—the realm of photons, electrons, and sub-atomic particles.

Unfortunately, detailed and rigorous experiments have proven that the observation and measurement of sub-atomic entities do, indeed, change them. Sub-atomic particles don't even seem to exist until someone observes or measures them! However absurd, however offensive to common sense, reality in the atomic and subatomic world appears so fragile, transitory, and statistical that humans can't measure or even view it without fundamentally changing what they measure or view.

Take light. Since the days of Isaac Newton, scientists have argued over whether light is a wave or a particle. In 1803, Thomas Young performed experiments that "proved" light was a wave. A century later, Albert Einstein performed experiments that "proved" light was a particle. Yet light can't be both a wave (which is spread out) and a particle (which is contained in one place).

Or can it?

The answer, from quantum physics, is that human interaction with light determines what characteristics light will have. The mere act of studying light changes it. By choosing their experiment, scientists can see what they want. If an experiment is set up to test wave-like properties, light will act like a wave; if the experiment is set up to test particle-like properties, light will act like a particle. Thus, in the quantum realm, "the observer plays a crucial role in determining the physical nature of what is being observed."[3]

Now, the incredible quantum world of subatomic particles isn't the realm of everyday human experience, what's called the classical realm, the realm in which we live, move, and have our being, the realm where reality affects us as much as, if not more, than we affect it. We confront a reality that's already there to meet us, not one that exists only because we view it or that exists in a certain way because we view it a certain way. We're scratched by Schrödinger's cat, not because our interaction with the cat caused it to exist, but because we stepped on its tail, which was already there before we mashed it.

On the other hand, recent events in the Christian world could almost lead one to think that Protestants are acting as if the statistical uncertainty of quantum physics does govern reality. For many Protestants, the Roman Catholic Church has become like entities in the quantum realm; these Protestants see what they want depending on how they view it.

Since the sixteenth century, when Protestants have looked at the Roman Catholic Church, they have seen one thing, the same thing—the antichrist, the harlot of Revelation 17, Babylon the Great, the beast of Revelation 13, and the persecuting little horn of Daniel 7 and 8. Viewing Rome through the lens of Scripture, Protestants all but unanimously viewed the papal system as the explicit manifestation of Paul's warning in Thessalonians: "Let no man deceive you by any means: for that day shall not come, except there come a falling away first, and that man of sin be revealed, the son of perdition; Who opposeth and exalteth himself above all that is called God, or that is worshipped; so that he as God sitteth in the temple of God, shewing himself that he is God" (2 Thessalonians 2:1-3). Protestantism was partially founded on the premise that the Roman papacy was the antichrist, a view firmly rooted in the biblical texts and one held by Protestants for hundreds of years.

"The prophecies concerning the Antichrist," wrote church historian Leroy Edwin Froom, "soon became the center of controversy, as the [Protestant] Reformers pointed the incriminating finger of prophecy, saying, Thou art the Man of Sin! Rome was declared to be the Babylon of the Apocalypse, and the papal pontiffs, in their succession, the predicted Man of Sin. Separation from the Church of Rome and its pontifical head therefore came to be regarded as a sacred, bounden duty. Christians were urged to obey the command, 'Come out of her, My people.' To them, this separation was separation not from Christ and His church but from Antichrist. This was the basic principle upon which the Reformers prosecuted their work from the beginning."[4]

Even a cursory look at Martin Luther's writings, such as the one titled, *Against the Roman Papacy As An Institution of the Devil,* proves how basic this belief was.[5] For Luther (according to historians Iserloh, Glazik, and Jedin) "the papal church is the demoniacal power described in Scripture as antichrist, which lasts to the end of days and is to be fought, not with weapons, but with the word and the Spirit."[6] Most other of the early Reformers, while agreeing on little else, agreed on this point regarding the identity of Rome.

For centuries after Luther, Protestants of all stripes, whatever their doctrinal differences, saw in Rome the antichrist power depicted—and blatantly condemned—in Scripture. Almost all nascent Protestant movements (usually formed by breaking away from other ones), when looking at Rome, its teaching, its official statements, and its practices and decrees, came to the same conclusion. Anglicans, Lutherans, Methodists, Baptists, Puritans, Presbyterians, Anabaptists, Congregationalists, you name it, all saw Rome as antichrist. Anti-Catholicism was so basic and fundamental that it often formed part of the Protestant creeds. For instance, the Second Scotch Confession of Faith (A.D. 1580) reads in part: "And theirfoir we abhorre and detest all contrare Religion and Doctrine; but chiefly all kynde of Papistrie in generall and particular head is, even as they are now damned and confronted by the word of God and Scotland. But in special, we detest and refuse the usurped authorities of the Romane Antichrist upon the Scriptures of God. . . ."[7] This belief regarding the "Romane Antichrist" was as fundamental to Protestantism as was justification by faith alone, and remained so well into the twentieth century.

But times have changed, even dramatically. Rome is no longer the antichrist, or even an apostate church that has perverted or lost the essential truths of salvation by faith alone. On the contrary, when many Protestants look at Roman Catholics, they see those with a "common understanding of salvation," who are "brothers and sisters in Christ." They see a "common faith" held by those with whom Protestants can "together bear witness to the gift of salvation." They see those who are "disciples together of the Lord Jesus Christ," those with whom they have "unity in the gospel." Some even now view the pope, whose mere existence was once an affront to biblical Christianity, as "the universal primate . . . to be received by all churches." Even in Adventism, the historical—and biblical—understanding of papal Rome has been questioned, which proves just how infectious this new perception has become.[8]

Quantum or classic?

What's happened here? Has Roman Catholicism become like light, and Protestants like scientists viewing it in the sub-atomic realm? Are people seeing merely what they want to see? Are Protestants choosing the means by which they look at Rome in order to "change" it into a reality that they want?

Rome has, it is true, changed in some dramatic ways. For example, since Vatican Council II the papacy has been bridging the gap between itself and other denominations, a radical shift from her previous antipathy to all those who were outside the "Mother Church." This is the age of pluralism, of nonjudgmentalism, of ecumenism, and tolerance and religious freedom, and Rome certainly is imbibing of this *zeitgeist.* Instead of openly attacking and denouncing Protestants and Protestant theology as (according to one pope) "the nefarious enterprises of wicked men, who, like raging waves of the sea foaming out their own confusion, and promising liberty whereas they are the slaves of corruption, have striven by their deceptive opinions and most pernicious writings to raze the foundations of the Catholic religion and of civil society, to remove from among men all virtue and justice, to deprave persons, and especially inexperienced youth, to lead it into the snares of error, and at length to tear it from the bosom of the Catholic Church"[9]—Rome is actively seeking reunion and unity with these once "nefarious" "slaves of corruption." In contrast to previous vicars, Pope John Paul II issued in 1995 an encyclical called *Ut Unum Sint* ("That They May Be One"), in which he passionately appealed for unity among all churches, saying that he longed for a day when "there may be one visible Church of God."[10]

Also, unlike his predecessors, John Paul II has published some of the clearest and most ringing statements about religious freedom ever published by anyone anywhere, claiming that "it is essential that the right to express one's own religious convictions publicly and in all domains of civil life be ensured" and that "people must not attempt to impose their own 'truth' on others"[11]—a big shift from the time when popes railed against liberty of conscience and religious freedom. In these areas, Rome has indeed made some radical, and undeniable, changes.

What Rome hasn't changed its position on, however, is the issue that started the Reformation itself—justification by faith alone, what the Reformers called "the article upon which the church stands or falls," "the first and chief article"[12] of faith, the "ruler and judge over all other Christian doctrines"—the exact issue that many Protestants are now claiming as the basis for unity with Rome!

It's amazing. However much Protestants are acting as if everyday reality functions at the quantum realm—the realm in which just viewing an object changes its characteristics—instead, what's happening is pure classical physics: it isn't the *object* that is changed by being observed, it's the *subject.* It's not what is being viewed that is altered, but the viewer himself. Protestants haven't opened the box and, by looking, created a live cat with sharp claws; instead, they have been unwittingly scratched, deeply, by claws that were already there to begin with.

Antichrist as the "body of Christ"

All one has to do is read, carefully, what Rome teaches her own people, and what practices she still espouses, in order to see that today she no more proclaims righteousness by faith, as taught by Paul and Luther, than she did in the sixteenth century when the Council of Trent formally rejected justification by faith alone and condemned the Reformation. Roman Catholic theology and dogma prove that Rome could never accept the gospel, as historically understood by Protestants, without radically reshuffling, revising, or undoing her most basic doctrines, which she has not done.

Nor does she need to. All Rome needs to do is sign a few documents with phraseology nebulous enough for each side to read into the texts what they want to read, and Protestants can proclaim unity with the same system that for centuries it labeled "antichrist." Antichrist has now become part of the body of Christ—without having to change a single essential doctrine. Rome is following one of the early thorns in her flesh, William of Occam, whose famous principle stated, *Why make things more complicated than they need be?* Why should Rome change any essentials when she doesn't have to? It's Protestants who are changing.

"Has Rome's position changed?" asked evangelical writer Michael Horton in the context of this new Protestant rush to claim unity with Rome. "In fact it has not. The Vatican II documents as well as the *New Catechism of the Catholic Church* reinvoke the theological position of the Council of Trent, condemning the gospel of justification by an imputed righteousness. If it is not Rome that has altered its position in favor of the gospel, then it must be the other partner that has moved from its earlier position."[13]

Horton sounds like Ellen White, who wrote: "It is not without reason that the claim has been put forth that Catholicism is now almost like Protestantism. There has been a change; but the change is in Protestants, not in Romanists."[14] She wrote these words more than a century before Protestants and Catholics were signing statements such as *Evangelical and Catholics Together: The Christian Mission in the Third Millennium,* in which evangelicals claimed that because Roman Catholics have the gospel, there was no need for Protestants to evangelize them.

What's happening here? Conservative Protestants, once Rome's most implacable foe, now claim unity with the papacy, not just over such issues as abortion, prayer in school, or pornography, but over justification by faith, the very issue that has divided them for centuries! Evangelical leaders in America write articles and books claiming that Roman Catholics and Protestants have the same understanding of salvation and justification by faith! Justification by faith alone, which once divided the two groups now suddenly unites them!

Twice in the 1990s conservative Protestants in the United States have signed documents claiming that Roman Catholics and Protestants agree on the essential elements of the gospel, of salvation by faith alone. And, in 1999 the Lutheran World Federation and Roman Catholics signed a *Joint Declaration on the Doctrine of Justification* in Augsburg, Germany, claiming "a consensus on basic truths of the doctrine of justification," which "shows that the remaining differences in its explication are no longer the occasion for doctrinal condemnations"[15] and therefore "the reasons for the rift in the sixteenth century is no longer applicable for the present moment."[16]

How can this be? Why are Protestants so eager to claim that Rome has a biblical understanding of salvation by faith alone, when it's obvious that Rome's doctrine of salvation is still anti-Christian in every form? When Catholics say that we are "saved by faith in Christ," or that we are "saved by grace alone," or that we are "justified by Christ alone," or that "Christ's righteousness alone gives us merit before God" do they mean the same thing that Protestants mean when they make the same statements? Or, instead, are Catholics using similar language to express radically different concepts, while Protestants—acting as if everyday reality mirrors the way things work in the quantum realm—are seeing in Rome what they want to see by selectively choosing just how they look at it?

The answer will be obvious.

Cat in the box

Schrödinger's cat left many questions unanswered in the quantum realm. (By the way, Schrödinger never actually did stick some hapless feline in a box filled with cyanide; it was just a "thought experiment.") Yet that was the whole point, to show problems with the idea that observers could change reality by viewing it. And one problem is this: When does reality shift from quantum to classical physics? It's one thing to try to measure an object only ten billionths of a centimeter in size and weighing a millionth part of a billion billionth of a gram. Observing or measuring something of that size could, conceivably, disturb (or even destroy) it. Most of us, however, don't deal with things that small, at least not consciously.

Nevertheless, observation and measurement—whatever they might do to what is observed at the quantum or classical level—*always* affects the observer. To look at Jupiter is to have photons of sunlight reflected off the Jovian atmosphere and surface, reach into the eye, and impinge upon the retina, which in turn converts light energy into nerve energy that streams into the brain as an electrical-chemical process that can leave permanent synaptic connections in the brain. We are indeed changed, to some degree, by what we perceive, measure, and observe.

The crucial question, then, is: What has happened to Protestants that, looking at Rome, they see something radically different than what's there? Unless Rome exists on the quantum realm, and thus changes when she is viewed, the change has to be in the observer himself, typical of classical, not quantum, physics. Something has happened to Protestants, something that, perhaps, cannot be explained by physics—quantum or classical. Though sociology, psychology, politics, and anthropology all come into play, the crucial factor, the one that can answer this question, is found, instead, in theology—particularly prophecy:

"And I saw one of his heads as it were wounded to death; and his deadly wound was healed: *and all the world wondered after the beast"* (Revelation 13:3, italics supplied).

---

1. Gribben, John. *In Search of Schrödinger's Cat: Quantum Physics and Reality* (New York: Bantam Books) 1984, p. 203.

2.Davies, Paul. *God & The New Physics* (New York: Touchstone Books) 1983, p. 114.

3. Gleiser, Marcelo. *The Dancing Universe: From Creation Myths to the Big Bang* (New York: Plume Books) 1997, p. 229.

4. Leroy Edwin Froom. *The Prophetic Faith of Our Fathers* (Hagerstown, Md.: Review and Herald Publishing Company) 1984, vol. II, p. 245.

5. See *Luther's Works.* Volume 55. Index. (Philadelphia: Fortress Press) 1986, p. 12.

6. Erwin Iserloh, Joseph Glazis, Hubert Jedin. *History of the Christian Church.* "Reformation and Counter Reformation," vol. 5 (New York: Seabury Press) 1980, p. 78.

7. Schaff, Philip. *The Creeds of Christendom,* vol. III. "The Evangelical Protestant Creeds" (Grand Rapids, Mich.:Baker Book House) 1983, p. 481.

8. See Reinder Bruinsma, "Adventists and Catholics: Prophetic Preview or Prejudice?" *Spectrum* Summer, 1999, pp. 45-52.

9. Pope Pius IX, Encyclical *Quanta Cura* 8, December 1864. Section 1.

10. *Ut Unum Sint* (Vatican City: Libreria Editrice Vaticana)1995, p. 11.

11. *Message of His Holiness Pope John Paul II For the Celebration of the World Day of Peace.* 1 January 1991, pp. 3, 4.

12. The Smalcald Articles, II, I; Book of Concord, 292.

13. Michael Horton, writing the forward to *Faith Alone,* R.C. Sproul (Grand Rapids, Mich.: Baker Books) 1995, p. 12.

14. *The Spirit of Prophecy*, vol. 4, p. 388.

15. "Joint Declaration On The Doctrine of Justification," Section 5.

16. Press Release, " 'Passing Joint Declaration' is a 'big day' for Lutherans" No. 8/89, <http:/www.lutheranworld.org/news/counce8.html>.

CHAPTER TWO

Strange Loops

One day the Children of God came to the General Conference. Known also as "The Family," the Children of God was a religious community inaugurated on the beaches of southern California in the nascent 1960s. Their leader, Moses David (née David Berg), died years ago, and though the Children of God are dissipating, a scattered remnant remains.

One unique feature of this religious tradition is an evangelistic technique called "Fishy Flirting," a euphemism for using sex, or the promise of it, to lure people into their pews (probably works better than vegetarian cooking classes or Revelation Seminars). Because the Children of God were having problems with certain governments that were not necessarily favorable to this specific expression of faith, and not enjoying the constitutional "right" of fishy flirting in these foreign lands as they do in the United States, some Family members wanted to talk to the religious liberty people at the General Conference for counsel and, maybe, help. (Counsel they got. Help? Forget it!) In the General Conference protocol lounge, they met—four Children of God and four Seventh-day Adventists.

In the midst of this bizarre dialogue, one of the Children of God, a middle-aged man, told his conversion story.

"I was living in England," he said. "I had money, a fancy car, girlfriends, everything, but I was empty inside. For months, Moses David tried to lead me to Jesus, but I would not listen. No matter what he did, I just was closed, nothing would reach my heart. Then one night Moses David gave me his wife—and that was when I learned about the love of Jesus."

Gary Ross, an associate in the department, the only one who responded, stated, "That is quite a testimony!"

But more than just a testimony, this man's "conversion" raises a crucial issue, one that cuts to the heart of the Catholic-Protestant divide, and that is—the question of authority. Who, or what, is the ultimate authority regarding questions of faith and salvation?

The issue isn't peripheral. Though the great controversy's earthly climax is manifested as the struggle of those who worship the beast and his image versus those who worship God (Revelation 13; 14), the real question is *authority.* Whom we worship reveals whom we accept as final authority—and we all have a final authority, even if nothing higher than our own lusts and lower passions.

In the context of this Child of God's Damascus Road experience in Moses David's bed, Ellen White's statement in *The Great Controversy* becomes particularly crucial: "In His word, God has committed to men the knowledge necessary for salvation. The Holy Scriptures are to be accepted as an authoritative, infallible revelation of His will. They are the standard of character, the revealer of doctrines, *and the test of experience*"[1] (italics supplied).

The point is this: to deny anyone his own personal experiences is almost as ridiculous as telling him he doesn't exist; he has to exist in order to be told that he doesn't. This man's experience can't be denied him; obviously, he had it.

The question isn't the experience itself, but the *interpretation.* If a dead person were to appear to a spiritualist and to an Adventist, the spiritualist and the Adventist are going to have radically different interpretations of what happened, no matter how similar the experience.

If all reality were judged only by the experience itself, if sense perceptions were the final arbiter of truth, then the moon does move along with a speeding car, objects do bend in water, and the sun journeys from horizon to horizon in about twelve hours every day. Because sense perceptions (and emotions) are so subjective, so liable to being misread and misunderstood, people need some sort of criteria to judge and interpret them. The crucial question is, What are those criteria?

For this specific Child of God, it obviously wasn't Scripture. If it were, he would have come to a radically different conclusion regarding what happened during his nocturnal epiphany with Moses David's wife. But, because the Bible wasn't his standard of character, wasn't the revealer of his doctrines and the *tester of his experience*—he interpreted his adultery, not as a sin, *but as a revelation of God's love in Christ*!

Whatever our beliefs about the cosmos and our place in it, we all live by some final authority, be it sacred writings, personal convictions, cultural traditions, social norms, familial bonds, unaided reason, carnal drives, or some combination thereof. Whatever, wherever, and however—the buck always stops somewhere.

For Seventh-day Adventists, that stopping point is the Bible. There's no "farther back." With the Bible, we've reached, as it were, the borders of revealed reality, what theologians call the *norma normans non normata.*[2] It's not like matter, which we can keep breaking down into smaller and smaller components (some physicists speculate that matter might even be infinitely divisible). Scripture, ideally, is the bottom-line, the ultimate authority in matters of faith and doctrine, even the aspects of faith and doctrine derived from individual experiences.

We got this conviction, of course, from the Protestant Reformers, who expressed it in the confessional statement *sola scriptura,* "Scripture alone"—which means, essentially, that the Bible is its own best interpreter, and that through prayerful study of the Word anyone can come to understand the truths necessary to salvation without the need for human philosophy or ecclesiastical authority. For the Reformers, the Bible was like the sun that needs no light from earth. It is sufficient, in and of itself, to provide all the requisite illumination. *Sola scriptura* became the foundational principle of the Reformation and remains, perhaps more than anything else, that which divides (or *divided?)* Protestants from Catholics.

Sola scriptura, however, didn't arise in a vacuum. The Reformers adopted it in opposition to the Church of Rome, which claimed that in addition to the Bible, authority rested in "sacred tradition" and in the magisterium (the teaching authority of the church). And, with these other sources of authority—Rome has all the requisite armaments to defend herself from her critics because she is starting from a different point than they are.

After all, how can anyone disprove a belief that's grounded in an ultimate authority different from his own? It's not likely that two people, one using Karl Marx's *Das Kapital* as his final authority, and one using Adam Smith's *Wealth of Nations,* will even accept each other's arguments, much less agree on fundamental economic principles. Whatever your source of authority, unless accepted as valid by the other person, any arguments you base on that authority—no matter how logical or true—will be of little avail. One might as well try using the Egyptian Book of the Dead to convince an Adventist that his view of the Sabbath is wrong.

This principle applies with Rome. Her other sources of authority enable her not only to hold positions that either contradict, or transcend, Scripture (or at least the Protestant interpretation of it) but to defend those positions with almost airtight logic. No wonder Rome is unambiguous about authority; she has to be—her existence as a church depends on it.

In his Encyclical *Fides et Ratio,* Pope John Paul II expressed Rome's position on authority and on *sola scriptura:* "One current widespread symptom of this fideistic tendency" he wrote, "is a 'biblicism' which tends to make the reading and exegesis of sacred Scripture the sole criterion of truth. In consequence, the word of God is identified with sacred Scripture alone, thus eliminating the doctrine of the Church, which the Second Vatican Council stressed quite specifically. Having recalled that the word of God is present both in Scripture and tradition, the Constitution *Dei Verbum* continues emphatically, 'Sacred tradition and sacred Scripture comprise a single sacred deposit of the word of God entrusted to the Church. Embracing this deposit and united with their pastors, the people of God remain faithful to the teaching of the apostles.' *Scripture, therefore, is not the Church's sole point of reference.* The 'supreme rule of her faith' derives from the unity which the Spirit has created between *sacred tradition, sacred Scripture, and the magisterium of the Church* in a reciprocity which means that none of the three can survive without the others"[3] (italics supplied).

The Constitution *Dei Verbum* (which the Pope quoted) also says: "It is clear, therefore, that sacred tradition, sacred Scripture, and the teaching authority of the Church, in accord with God's most wise design, are so linked and joined together that one cannot stand without the others, and that all together and each in its own way under the action of the one Holy Spirit contribute effectively to the salvation of souls."[4]

In the official *Catechism of the Catholic Church,* released in the 1990s, John Paul II reiterated Rome's position: "A catechism should faithfully and systematically present the teaching of sacred Scripture, the living tradition in the Church and the authentic magisterium, as well as the spiritual heritage of the fathers, doctors, and saints of the church . . . . *The Catechism of the Catholic Church,* which I approved June 25th last and the publication of which I today ordered by virtue of my apostolic authority, is a statement of the church's faith and of catholic doctrine, attested to or illuminated by sacred Scripture, the apostolic tradition, and the Church's magisterium. I declare it to be a sure norm for teaching the faith and thus a valid and legitimate instrument for ecclesiastical communion." The Pope then beseeched "the blessed Virgin Mary, mother of the incarnate Word and mother of the Church, to support with her powerful intercession the catechetical work of the entire church on every level."[5]

The *Catechism* itself is unequivocal: "Sacred tradition and sacred Scripture make up a single sacred deposit of the Word of God."[6]

Two points scream out from these statements. First, Rome rejects the fundamental position of Protestantism, *sola scriptura,* the starting point on which it bases its entire theological foundation. John Paul is unambiguous: "Scripture, therefore, is *not* the Church's sole point of reference" (italics supplied). For Protestants, however, Scripture *is* the sole reference point.

This basic difference on authority cannot be underestimated; from this difference over authority the Protestant-Catholic divide finds its roots, origins, and reasons for existence.

What is truth?

From the start, then, Protestants and Catholics are working from different premises. It's like an orchestra with the brass, percussion, and woodwinds playing from one score, while the strings and pianos are, simultaneously, playing from another. Though harmony is possible, it's not very likely.

The pope said that besides "sacred Scripture" there is "sacred tradition" and the magisterium, none of which can "survive without the others." The implication of those words should cause Protestants to flee Rome, not embrace its adherents as "brothers and sisters in Christ." If Scripture can't survive without tradition or the magisterium, then Rome either lowers Scripture or elevates tradition and the magisterium, to levels that no true Protestant could accept.

The magisterium is "the perennial, authentic, and infallible teaching office committed to the apostles of Christ and now possessed and exercised by their legitimate successors, the college of bishops in union with the pope."[7] Though Rome has modified its precise understanding of the role and function of its teaching office, the magisterium consists basically of church leaders, under the supreme authority of the pope, answering Pilate's famous question, "What is truth?"

For the magisterium, two basic sources of truth exist, "sacred tradition" and "sacred Scripture." Tradition (whose literal meaning is "hands on") is Rome's process of passing on teachings to the faithful. Derived from history, the church fathers, and what it believes is a corpus of oral truths, "sacred tradition" is both the filter through which the magisterium interprets the Bible and also the process by which it promulgates it. Rome defines tradition as such: "The Church, in her teaching, life, and worship, perpetuates and hands on to all generations all that she herself is, all the she believes."[8]

The issue regarding "sacred tradition" leads to the crux of the Protestant-Catholic chasm: Protestants say *sola scriptura;* Catholics say *scriptura* and "sacred tradition" (as interpreted by the magisterium). This difference leads Catholics and Protestants to radically different conclusions on almost every aspect of Christian faith.

The problem even gets more complicated because, though some statements show that Rome places "sacred Scripture," "sacred tradition," and the magisterium on the same level—other sources assert that "sacred tradition" and the magisterium are defined and controlled by Scripture. If this latter statement is true, the equation changes dramatically; in that case, Rome would not, really, differ from Protestants on the key issue of authority.

"[T]he authority," says the *Catholic Encyclopedia,* "of the magisterium is a relative authority. Entirely derived from the authoritative mission given by Christ to the apostles . . . it is relative to, and bound by, the authority of the revealed Word itself."[9]

If the magisterium is bound by the authority of the Bible itself, what's the problem? What makes the Catholic magisterium any different from Protestants whose churches often have their own teaching bodies that interpret truth, ideally, through the Scriptures? Also, doesn't an official, centralized teaching authority provide a better way to formulate doctrine than having hordes of Bible-spouting would-be exegetes, each declaring revealed "truth" that constantly conflicts with each other, as happens in Protestantism?

In fact, Rome claims that even "sacred tradition" must be tested by Scripture. "The Church controls verifies, proves, and even criticizes her tradition by Scripture."[10] Again, what's wrong with this—especially since Protestants, too, have their own traditions that they also claim to test by the Bible?

In short, what's wrong with either tradition or a teaching authority if all things are verified, proved, even criticized by Scripture?

Nothing, except that to say the teaching authority and "sacred tradition" are subject to the Word of God is essentially meaningless. Why? Because the Word of God has to be interpreted, and in the Roman Church it is interpreted by the teaching authority *using sacred tradition as its guide.* The Constitution *Dei Verbum* states that "sacred tradition takes the Word of God entrusted by Christ the Lord and the Holy Spirit to the apostles and hands it on to their successors in its *full purity,* so that led by the light of the Spirit of truth, they may in proclaiming it preserve this Word of God faithfully, explain it, and make it more widely known"[11] (italics supplied).

How can "sacred tradition" be tested by the Bible when the Bible is, itself, interpreted in "its full purity" by "sacred tradition"? Also, what does it mean for the magisterium to be "bound" by the Word of God when the magisterium itself interprets the Word of God? One is hardly bound who determines the size, degree, and scope of his own bonds.

It's a classic case of "which came first, the chicken or the egg?" Rome claims that its tradition is tested by Scripture, but the Scripture is interpreted through tradition. How can tradition be criticized by the Bible when tradition itself determines how the Bible is interpreted? Tradition is tested by Scripture; but Scripture is interpreted by tradition, which is tested by the Scripture, which is interpreted by tradition, which is tested by Scripture. . . .

It's like the "canos per tonos" in Bach's *Musical Offering,* where through a series of tonal modulations Bach brings the music in a circle of notes until the listener ends where he started, over and over again. In W. C. Escher's famous 1961 lithograph, *The Waterfall,* the source of the waterfall winds up in the same place it ends; no matter how many times you follow the water through its course, it always ends where it begins. Douglas Hofstadter called the phenomenon "Strange Loops," which occur "whenever, by moving upwards (or downwards) through levels of some hierarchical system, we unexpectedly find ourselves right back where we started."[12] This is what happens in Roman Catholic theology regarding Scripture, authority, and interpretation.

For instance, when John Paul, in the introduction to the *Catechism of the Catholic Church,* thanked the Virgin Mary for "her powerful intercession [in] the catechetical work of the entire church on every level"—where did he get the idea that Mary can now intercede in behalf of the church?

From the Bible, of course. After all, doesn't Scripture record the angel saying to Mary "thou *that art highly favoured,* the Lord is with thee: *blessed art thou among women"* (Luke 1:28)? Doesn't the Scripture record her cousin Elisabeth, "filled with the Holy Ghost," saying to Mary: *"Blessed art thou among women,* and blessed is the fruit of thy womb" (Luke 1:42)? And doesn't Mary herself in the Holy Scriptures exclaim: "My soul doth magnify the Lord, And my spirit hath rejoiced in God my Saviour. For he hath regarded the low estate of his handmaiden: *for, behold, from henceforth all generations shall call me blessed. For he that is mighty hath done to me great things"* (Luke 1:46-48, italics supplied)?

What great things did the Lord do for Mary? Letting her carry the infant Jesus is, certainly, one. What else? The answer depends on interpretation. Though these verses don't deny that Mary could one day be an intercessor in heaven, the repeated promises of divine blessings on her could be interpreted, through the lens of tradition, to mean that she would be such an intercessor. How do you know the tradition is right? You test it (as Rome says) by the text. How do you know your interpretation of the text is right? You interpret it through the lens of tradition. How do you know the tradition is right? You test it by the text. How do you know your interpretation of the text is right? You interpret it through the lens of tradition.

Strange loops, indeed.

To claim that the texts don't say anything about Mary being an intercessor begs the point. How do you know that they don't say that? You have to interpret the texts. How do you interpret them—from our private judgment, as Protestants teach, or by the long and revered tradition of the church built up over centuries and centuries of study and prayer by some of the greatest names in Christian history, as Rome teaches? (Of course, both groups claim the leading of Holy Spirit, so bringing Him in answers nothing here.)

Rome has, unambiguously, given its reply: Scripture is interpreted through "the living tradition in the Church and the authentic magisterium, as well as the spiritual heritage of the fathers, doctors, and saints of the church . . ."

Protestants, however, face the same epistemological conundrum as do Catholics. We claim not to be bound, as are Catholics, to tradition (though Protestants certainly have their own traditions) because we interpret the Scripture in a way that doesn't exalt tradition as does Rome. But how do we know that our interpretation is correct and Rome's isn't? We use our own judgment. What makes us think that our own judgment is right? We test it by the Bible. But how do we interpret the Bible? By our own judgment. But how do we know our judgment is right? We test it by the Bible. . . .

Strange loops, again?

The point, at least here, isn't to criticize Rome's "sacred tradition." Any Protestant must reject it outright as contradictory to the Protestant understanding of what the Bible means. The point, instead, is to show that—despite the gooey and loving pronouncements about "unity in the Lord" and "a common understanding of salvation"—if each side sticks to its own authority, and those authorities conflict, then the divide between them remains impenetrable. Catholics and Protestants are working from two different Periodic Tables of Elements—not exactly the best way to do chemistry. If you can't agree on your sources of authority, and if each side's authority contradicts the axioms, postulates, and formulas of the other's, any claims of unity should be powerfully suspect.

Indeed, despite all the effusive documents, enthusiastic statements, and smiling pronouncements to the contrary, Protestants and Catholics are divided asunder on the most basic issue that can divide anyone—and that is authority. "The age-long controversy between Protestantism and Roman Catholicism," wrote Protestant scholar Loraine Boettner, "comes to a head regarding the question of authority."[13] Thus, as long as Rome won't budge on "sacred tradition" and Protestants stand fast on *sola scriptura*—any claim for unity is like Lazarus before Jesus spoke life into his corpse: It "stinketh."

A common Bible?

However differently they interpret the Bible, Protestants and Catholics at least agree that the Bible is the Word of God, a commonality that they don't share with Trotskyites, animists, and members of the Aum Shinrikyo. *Evangelicals and Catholics Together: The Christian Mission in the Third Millennium,* signed in 1993, claims: "We affirm together that Christians are to teach and live in obedience to the divinely inspired Scriptures, which are the infallible Word of God."[14]

However good that commonality sounds, there's one slight problem—each group has a different "infallible Word of God." Catholics have added fourteen books to their Bible that didn't make the King James Version, or just about any other Protestant version. Known as the *Apocrypha,* from which the word "apocryphal" arises (used to refer to something dubious), these books have been excluded by Protestants from the Bible, and with good reasons. Whatever their historical or literary value, books such as Susanna, Bell and the Dragon, Tobit, Judith, and Baruch, among others, are filled with nonsense.

Take, for instance, Tobit—included in the Roman Catholic "infallible Word of God"—which tells this story: "The boy left with the angel, and the dog followed behind. The two walked on, and when the first evening came they camped besides the Tigris. The boy had gone down to the rise to wash his feet, when a great fish leaped out of the water and all but swallowed his foot. The boy gave a shout and the angel said, 'Catch the fish, do not let it go.' The boy mastered the fish and pulled it onto the bank. The angel said, 'Cut it open; take out the gall, the heart, and the liver; set these aside and throw the entrails away, for the gall and heart and liver have curative properties' . . . Then the boy asked the angel this question, 'Brother Azaria, what can the fish's heart, liver, and gall cure?' He replied, 'You burn the fish's heart and liver, and their smoke is used in the case of a man or woman plagued by a demon or evil spirit; any such affliction leaves for good, leaving no trace. As regards to the gall, this is used as an eye ointment for anyone having white spots on his eyes; after using it, you only have to blow on the white spots to cure them' " (Tobit 6:1-5, 7-9, Jerusalem Bible).

Along with Hebrews 11, Romans 3, 1 Corinthians 13, Exodus 20, and Genesis 22—there's Tobit 6, part of the "infallible Word of God," which Catholics and Protestants claim as a basis of unity between them?

Those who signed *Evangelicals and Catholics Together* signed a string of words saying that both Catholics and Protestants believe the Bible is "the infallible Word of God." Yet what can a string of words about a common belief in the "infallible Word of God" mean when one group includes in that "infallible Word" texts that the other group rejects as, literally, apocryphal?

The statement from *Evangelicals and Catholics Together* saying, "We affirm together that Christians are to teach and live in obedience to the divinely inspired Scriptures, which are the infallible Word of God," exemplifies how Catholics and Protestants can sign these documents—and in good conscience, too—despite contradictory theologies, methods of interpretations, and terminal sources of authority. When Catholics say the "the infallible Word of God," and when Protestants say the "infallible Word of God," though using the same terms, they just mean different things, that's all.

And it's this type of semantic fogginess that represents the metaphysic of all these documents—common words, but with different meanings to the words. Because all that Catholics and Protestants have in common are words, nothing else, and certainly not meanings. Considering the semantic trickery that they performed with something as concrete as the "infallible Word of God" itself, it's not hard to imagine what they do with abstract theological terms such as "grace alone," "justification by faith," "righteousness by faith," "salvation," "merit," "imputed righteousness" and "the gospel."

The bottom line, again, is authority. Catholicism and Protestantism, though sharing a common theological vocabulary, are really different religions with different premises because *they have different sources of authority.* The semantic blurriness of these ecumenical statements masks what is really a profound existential and theological division, a division as great as the one between truth and error, between light and darkness—indeed, between Christ and antichrist itself.

---

1. *The Great Controversy,* p. vii.

2. "The norm which is the standard for all other norms but is not itself subject to a higher norm."

3. *Fides et Ratio,* pp. 23, 24. September 14, 1998.

4. *DEI VERBUM* (DOGMATIC CONSTITUTION ON DIVINE REVELATION.) N. 10.

5. *Catechism of the Catholic Church,* "Apostolic Constitution" (New York: Doubleday) 1995, pp. 4-7.

6. Catechism of the Catholic Church, (CCC) #97.

7. *Catholic Encyclopedia,* vol. 13, "Teaching Authority of the Church," 1967, p. 959.

8. *DEI VERBUM* , n.10.

9. *Catholic Encyclopedia,* vol. 13, p. 961.

10. *Catholic Encyclopedia,* vol.14, p. 227.

11. *DEI VERBUM,* n. 9.

12. Douglas Hofstadter, *Gödel, Escher, Bach* (New York: Vintage Books) 1979, p.10.

13. Boettner, Loraine. *Roman Catholicism* (Phillipsburg, N.J.: Presbyterian and Reformed Publishing Company) 1962, p. 75.

14. *Evangelicals and Catholics Together.* Introduction, March 29, 1993.

CHAPTER THREE

How Are We Saved?

In *Gulliver's Travels,* Jonathan Swift (1667-1745) wrote about the long war between "the two great empires of Lilliput and Blefuscu"[1] over which end of an egg should be broken—the big or the little end. According to earliest historical accounts, when the grandfather of Lilliput's present king broke open an egg in the traditional manner, that is, on the big end, he cut his finger. "Whereupon the Emperor his father published an edict commanding all his subjects, upon great penalties, to break the smaller end of their eggs."[2] Some, highly resentful of the edict, revolted and fled to Blefuscu, whose leaders were constantly egging on these dissenters (known as "Big-Endians") in their refusal to stop breaking eggs on the large end. Eventually war broke out between Lilliput and Blefuscu; thousands died, and many ships were sunk. Though the holy prophet Lustrog said that "all true believers shall break their eggs on the convenient end," and Gulliver, a witness to the turmoil, added that the convenient end should be "left to every man's conscience, or at least in the power of the chief magistrate to determine"[3]—neither side would concede even a millimeter. The emperor of Lilliput then wanted the giant Gulliver to destroy the Big-Endian exiles and force all Blefuscudians to "break the smaller end of their eggs."[4] Gulliver refused, and the emperor never forgave him.

Swift's satire, however absurd, mocked the difference between Protestants and Catholics, differences that led them to shed each other's blood in the name of Him who, because He "laid down his life for us," said that "we ought to lay down our lives for the brethren," (1 John 3:16)—*not* that we ought to lay down our brethren's lives for Him, which is exactly what those who fought these wars thought they were doing. And though no one could justify killing another over *any* doctrine (especially in the name of the Prince of Peace), the question does remain: Just how big were, and are, the differences between Roman Catholic and Protestant theology regarding salvation by faith?

Are they—as men such as Charles Colson, Pat Robertson, Keith Fournier, and others suggest—on a par with whether to break the small or large end of an egg? Or is there something else at stake, something profound, something crucial, something terminally true?

Are the differences that have caused this long, painful, hateful, and at times, bloody divide between Protestants and Catholics merely disputes over semantics? "We realized," said one Lutheran participant in *The Joint Declaration* discussions, that "we were not as far apart as we thought, that we were just using different vocabularies."[5] Or, are the differences merely over theological trivialities? "We must lay aside minor doctrinal differences," said Pat Robertson regarding Catholic and Protestant unity.[6]

Or, instead, are the differences major, fundamental, and crucial—the differences, in fact, between Christ and antichrist?

Though the questions can appear deep, complicated, couched under a profusion of theological locutions such as *sola fide,* concupiscence, *cooperatio,* forensic and infused (or for that matter, imputed and imparted) righteousness, *simul istus et peccator,* expiation, extra-sacramental remission, sanctification, *iustitia alienum,* plenary indulgences, regeneration, and on and on—it all can be pared down, even purified, into one question: *How are we saved?*

However simple, that question reigns as the most important in any person's life because, in the end, no matter what august letters may be annexed to a person's name, no matter how many figures to the left of the decimal point a person's bank account may begin with, no matter how many faces may recognize his face in a crowd, if a person is not saved, if he or she doesn't receive immortality at the end of the age, then everything else—the letters, the numbers, the recognition—all becomes meaningless. Without salvation, all that anyone has ever done, accomplished, or said will all be ash—even less, for not even ash survives. Only the saved will survive the end of this world. All else, everyone else—is gone, purged by the cleansing fire of a God who will wipe the slate clean and begin again with nothing from this world except the souls saved out of it.

Thus, *How are we saved?* isn't mere religious philosophizing, akin to speculating upon the hylomorphic nature of angels or upon Anselm's ontological argument for the existence of God. Rather, this question gets to the core of all that it means to be human, of all that it means to be a sinner, of all that it means to be right with our Creator. To answer this question is to create the axiom upon which all other proofs, syllogisms, theories, and formula rest. Once this question is answered, everything else is superscript.

Justification by faith

How are we saved?

To rephrase it in the immediate context of the ever-diminishing Protestant-Catholic divide: Either we are justified by what Christ has done *for* us, apart from anything else—including what He does in us—or we're not. Expressed as such, the issue allows for no middle ground, no mediating compromise, no golden mean because none exists—and to assume not only that some middle ground exists, but that it can be extracted through cordial, loving, and open dialogue, is to be either saying or believing a lie. You might as well believe that cordial, loving, and open dialogue will lead to a compromise position between those who say that George Washington was the first president of the United States and those who deny it. Either George was, or he wasn't. Either 2 + 2 = 4 (in the base ten number system) or it doesn't. Either the sum of the squares of the lengths of the sides of a right triangle is equal to the square of the length of the hypotenuse (in Euclidian geometry), or it's not. Either justification is totally by what Christ has done *for us*, *outside* of us—or it's not.

If justification, in any way, includes something that happens *in us*, then we are not "justified by what Christ has done *for* us, apart from anything else, *including what He does in us.*" It can't be both any more than 2 + 2 can equal 4 and not equal 4 at the same time. Either justification is, as Protestant theologian Alister McGrath writes, "the forensic *declaration* that the Christian is righteous, rather than the process by which he or she is *made* righteous. It involves a change in *status* rather than in *nature*"[7] (italics his)—or justification is, as the new *Catechism of the Catholic Church (CCC),* says "the remission of sins, sanctification, and the renewal of the inner man."[8] Either, as Ellen White says, "it is not possible to effect anything in our standing before God or in the gift of God to us through creature merit"[9] or, as the CCC says, "moved by the Holy Spirit, we can merit for ourselves and for others all the graces needed to attain eternal life."[10] Either, as Martin Luther wrote, "faith alone, without works, justifies, frees, and saves,"[11] or as the Council of Trent said, "If anyone says that the sinner is justified by faith alone, meaning that nothing else is required to cooperate in order to obtain the grace of justification . . . let him be anathema."[12]

These positions exclude each other; one can't be right without disqualifying the other. One says that justification is only what happens outside of us; the other says that justification happens outside *and* inside us. One or the other statement can be true, or maybe neither is true, but certainly both can't be true. The Catholic belief that justification *includes* what happens outside us doesn't make it Protestant any more than a cannibal's taste for broccoli makes him vegetarian.

The difference between Catholics and Protestants over justification isn't quantitative; it's not a matter of degree or line-drawing or of occupying a different spot on the same continuum. The lines are perpendicular, not parallel; that they might cross in one spot means only that they're moving in different directions, not that they've found grounds for harmony. Justification is either 100 percent based on something outside of us, or it is not. If it's not, then the Catholics are right; if it is, then the Protestants are. Both groups can't be right—despite these documents' bogus claims that both are.

Far from revealing theological harmony between Catholics and Protestants, what these documents reveal, instead, is the harmony between what Adventists have warned would someday happen in the Christian world and what is, in fact, happening today. Masterpieces of linguistic ambiguity and theological obfuscation such as *Evangelicals and Catholics Together,* the *Gift of Salvation,* and *The Joint Declaration on the Doctrine of Justification,* not counting the papal encyclical *Ut Unum Sint* (in which the pope calls for unity with all churches), are dramatically fulfilling the words of Ellen White, who wrote more than a century ago that "Romanism is now regarded by Protestants with far greater favor than in former years. In those countries where Catholicism is not in the ascendancy, and the papists are taking a conciliatory course in order to gain influence, there is an increasing indifference concerning the doctrines that separate the reformed churches from the papal hierarchy; *the opinion is gaining ground that, after all, we do not differ so widely upon vital points as has been supposed,* and that a little concession on our part will bring us into a better understanding with Rome. The time was when Protestants placed a high value upon the liberty of conscience which had been so dearly purchased. They taught their children to abhor popery and held that to seek harmony with Rome would be disloyalty to God. But how widely different are the sentiments now expressed!"[13] (italics supplied).

The finest standards of faith

This transition is one of the most profound since Copernicus's *Di Revolutionibus* put the sun, not the earth, at the center of our solar system. After centuries, the Counter-Reformation has born fruit beyond Ignatius Loyola's wildest dreams. Rome's theologians have succeeded where her dungeon-keepers failed. When you have a person's mind, why bloody your hands with his body?

After all, who needs the stake or the rack when Billy Graham, the world's most famous evangelical, utters, "I have found that my beliefs are essentially the same as those of orthodox Roman Catholics"[14]? Reverend Graham's use of the word "orthodox" is revelatory; it represents a major theological realignment among evangelicals who now stress that they have more in common with conservative Catholics—those who strictly adhere to Rome's teachings—than they do with liberals within Rome's massive fold.

This trend was crudely, if not enthusiastically, expressed in a video *(Startling Revelations: Pope John Paul II)* by Protestant evangelist Jack Van Impe, in which he quotes 2 Thessalonians 2:3—"Let no man deceive you by any means: for that day shall not come, except there come a falling away first, and that man of sin be revealed, the son of perdition," a verse that echoed for centuries as the Protestant mantra identifying the pope and the papal apostasy as antichrist. Van Impe, however, in one of the most perverse apocalyptic twists of the twentieth century, used that text (and other similar ones) to refer to the liberal theologians in the Catholic Church fighting *against* the pope. For Van Impe, Paul's predicted "falling away" wasn't the rise of the papacy—the standard (and correct) Protestant view since Martin Luther. Rather, the "falling away" is represented by liberal Catholics in the Roman Church who are unfaithful to papal teachings or to John Paul's "conservatism on morals and doctrine." Warning listeners that these "apostates" could be part of the antichrist power itself, Van Impe commends the pope for exposing them as such.

"Protestants," said Van Impe, "have literally been flabbergasted to know that the pope is right on target concerning this final, end-time event."

"Historic" is the term commonly used to describe this monumental change; "prophetic" of course, is more accurate, but these evangelicals—so alienated from the historicist interpretation of Scripture—are too ignorant of prophecy to understand how they are following the script broadly brushed out in the pages of Revelation (not to mention *The Great Controversy,* where Ellen White warned, with incredible foresight: "Protestants have tampered with and patronized popery; they have made compromises and concessions which papists themselves are surprised to see and fail to understand. Men are closing their eyes to the real character of Romanism and the dangers to be apprehended from her supremacy"[15]).

Mark A. Noll, MacManis Professor of Christian Thought at Wheaton College (and, ironically enough, editor of a book called *The Confessions and Catechisms of the Reformation*) wrote: "Catholics and evangelicals recognize that it is as best dubious, and at worst simply wrong, for Catholics and evangelicals to proselytize across the Catholic-Protestant border in situations where believers are coming close to *the finest standards* of either faith"[16] (italics supplied).

Evangelicals should not try to convert devout Catholics, those who represent the "finest standards" of their faith, because, essentially, these Catholics have so much in common with evangelicals already? It's like saying that Christians shouldn't witness to Jews because—believing in Moses, Jeremiah, and Isaiah—Jews have more in common with evangelicals than they do with cannibals, animists, and Marxist-Leninists.

Noll's words are seismic. The contrast between the "finest standards" of the Roman Catholic faith and Protestantism puts each irrefutably *at odds* with the other on the most fundamental issue of all, *How are we saved?* One might as well not give penicillin to someone with the purest, greatest strain of syphilis because, after all, both disease and cure are bacterial. That many Roman Catholics are fine individual believers is, utterly, irrelevant (many fine Hindus exist too; that hardly makes their religion true).

In fact, the "finest standards" of Roman Catholic theology place it in direct, irreconcilable opposition to everything that Protestantism and the Reformation represent. For Noll and other Protestants to miss this point exposes an incredible theological/sociological (and prophetic) shift. The more faithfully one adheres to Catholic theology regarding justification, the more the gospel is usurped. The more loyal one is to Rome, the more disloyal one is to biblical truth. The more one follows the Roman Catholic view of salvation, the further one gets from the Cross. Once this scandalous, religiously incorrect, and "bigoted" truth is understood, the bogusness of those recently-signed documents, the darkness of contemporary Protestantism, and the treasonous deception of Noll's words about "the finest standards of either faith" will be exposed in all their pernicious shadows, penumbras, and fallacious shades.

And that's what *The Great Compromise* does, it exposes these pernicious and fallacious linguistic shades. For, contrary to the propaganda, which causes the unwary to think that the difference between Protestants and Catholics on salvation is nothing more important than which end of the egg to break, these differences, instead, get to the heart of the only question that matters, the one question that makes all other questions fade into trivia—and that is, *How are we saved?*

---

1. Jonathan Swift. *Gulliver's Travels* (New York: Bantam Books) 1981, p. 62.
2. Swift. pp. 62, 63.
3. Swift. p. 63.
4. Swift. p. 66.
5. *Washington Post,* November 1, 1999. A24.
6. Quoted in James R. Wallis Jr. "Historic Christian Declaration Signed" *Christian American,* May/June 1994. p.4.
7. Alister McGrath *Justification by Faith* (Grand Rapids, Mich.:Baker Academic Books) 1988, p .61.
8. *Catechism of the Catholic Church.* Para. 2019.
9. *Faith and Works,* p. 19.
10. *Catechism of the Catholic Church* Para. 2027.
11. Quoted in Garret Ward Sheldon, ed. *Religion and Politics* (New York: Peter Lang) 1990, pp. 62.
12. *Canons and Decrees of the Council of Trent* (Rockford, Ill.: Tan Books) 1978, Can. 9.
13. *Great Controversy,* p. 563.
14. Quoted in R.C. Sproul, *Faith Alone*: *The Evangelical Doctrine of Justification* (Grand Rapids, Mich.: Baker Books) 1995, p. 11.
15. *The Great Controversy,* p. 566.
16. *Evangelicals and Catholics Together,* Charles Colson, Richard John Neuhaus, Eds. (Dallas: Word Publishing) 1995. Mark. A. Knoll. "The History of an Encounter" pp. 105, 106.

CHAPTER FOUR

Wormholes

Maybe opposites attract in physics, but not in religious faith, where opposites repel. That's why, for almost five hundred years, Catholics and Protestants repelled one another like two negative electrical charges. Honest, open about their differences, and living at a time when the *concept* of truth was taken more seriously than it is today, both sides realized that no ground for unity existed, particularly on the nature of justification. For example, at the Council of Trent (still viewed as authoritative by Rome), the Vatican explicitly *condemned* justification by faith alone and cursed those who accepted it.

"If anyone says that the sinner is justified by faith alone," said the council, "meaning that nothing else is required to cooperate in order to obtain the grace of justification . . . let him be anathema."[1]

Some Protestants, however, aren't going to let a mere detail such as an official condemnation of their most cherished doctrine hinder the hormonal urge to embrace Rome. This blind, passionate lurch toward Rome explains why an evangelical such as Mark Noll could say that evangelicals and Catholics shouldn't convert those who hold to "the finest standards of either faith"—even if "the finest standards of either faith" have placed both groups in irreconcilable theological opposition to each other.

There's no question that this shift in attitude represents one of the most dramatic manifestations of prophetic fulfillment since the beast was first "wounded to death" (Revelation 13:3) more than two hundred years ago. The wound is mending—and Protestant evangelicals are now supplying the "healing touch."

Noll's statement, however ludicrous, is nevertheless worth examining. What are "the finest standards of either faith" that bring Catholics and Protestants into such harmony that there's no need to try to convert each other? Only by looking at these "finest standards" can one realize how incredible, prophetic, and fallacious Noll's words really are.

The problem of sin

For Protestantism, the "finest standard" begins with justification by faith alone, the truth that answers the crucial question, *How are we saved?* The correct reply to the question reveals Christ in His matchless love and unfathomable grace, as well as exposes antichrist in all its deception and usurpation of that love and grace. The Protestant Reformers had this truth burned in their bones; time, however, has so diluted it that their children, far from carrying the torch, are raining on it watered-down doctrine instead.

How are we saved? This question can be answered only when one understands how we were lost, which is because of sin—the most damaging, destructive, and pernicious force in creation. It's hard for us, as sinners, to recognize what we're so steeped in. How do we objectively perceive that which has, in a sense, changed the very rhythms of the fermions and bosons that make up our being and all accessible physical reality? Sin so pervades our nature, so infects our thoughts, so filters what we see, hear, feel, and sense that trying to understand it fully is like trying to find shadows amid darkness. If every sin dulls our senses even more to its character, then we who live where sin is glorified, rewarded, and sanctified, where sin is as easy and as natural as breathing, where sin is what we "are," not just what we do—how can we be anything but numb and morally anaesthetized toward it? Almost all that is human—homes, schools, jobs, institutions, churches, relationships—do not exist as they do without being either radically affected, or even created, by sin. How can we understand sin when the very thought processes we use to understand it are already irreparably contaminated and damaged by it? It's like trying to dry off with water.

Nevertheless, the horizontal tragedies of sin are everywhere apparent, sucking life out of us from the moment our first two cells meet, mate, and make us what we are even before we become it. In every cry, every chancre, in every broken bone, and in every broken home—sin is the culprit. War, crime, perversion, oppression, these are surface reflections alone. Sin (not bad parenting) turns the soft cooing of a baby into the alluring charm of a child-molester years later. Sin (not wrong books) turns the sincerity of a fertile mind into the doubt of a cold skeptic. Sin (not the soldier) pulls the trigger of a gun. There's not a sorrow, a loss, or a scar rooted and grounded in anything but sin—ours or someone else's or everyone else's (it hardly matters whose). What matters is that sin *is,* and that every moment all who breathe suffer its consequences.

Yet the real tragedy of sin isn't in the horizontal, in that which siphons life from every cell, in that which has disturbed the harmony of the four dimensions, in that which makes every heart beat one closer to its final screaming, desperate spasm. The most basic, metaphysical consequences of sin exist in a realm we can access only by faith, never by sight or by touch or by reason. What we see, feel, and reason are only echoes, ripples, reflections of a deeper problem in a deeper reality. The real tragedy of sin exists in the vertical, in the rupture between heaven and earth, in the chasm between the creature and Creator. All that sin causes us to do to ourselves and to each other is because of what sin has done to our relationship with God. Sin ruptured that relationship, caused an estrangement, and created a division between the Creator and the created so that created became separated from the only Source of his existence, life, and purpose—

a separation with consequences more dire than if the umbilical cord were severed in the womb, because what the created lost because of sin wasn't just physical, but spiritual—even eternal.

First and foremost, then, it was to heal this infinite and eternal rift that Jesus Christ came and died, because until that vertical tear between heaven and earth was fixed, nothing else mattered. Faith, works, sanctification, holiness, the law, obedience, repentance, the Word, all these would have been meaningless, empty, void gestures akin to preaching sermons to—or stuffing food into the mouth of—a corpse. Nothing that happens *in* us or *to* us could have any lasting or eternal consequences until something first happened *for us,* something that we could never do for ourselves, and that was to restore sinful, degraded creatures back to favor with an infinitely pure and holy Creator.

Without delving deeply into fruitless metaphysical speculations about God, His essential nature, or the limits of His omnipotence (yes, even omnipotence has limits)—there's something about our Creator that *can't* (as opposed to *won't*) accept sin. *Won't* implies that He could if He chose to; yet if He could have accepted sin, He probably would have, because that would have spared Himself and Christ the infinite sufferings of the Cross. But God didn't accept sin because His ultimate nature, and the nature of the universe He has created, *can't* accept it—and the reason is that God is holy, *perfectly* holy. Now, if something, whatever it is, is *perfectly* that thing, then by nature it allows for nothing imperfect. An imperfection, to any degree, renders it imperfect. A perfect circle has to be everywhere equidistant from the center; if it were anywhere uneven, not matter how minutely, it could still be a circle, just not a perfect one. The same with God; if He's holy, then He's perfectly holy, and perfect holiness, by definition, allows for no unholiness.

"For thus saith the high and lofty One that inhabiteth eternity, whose name is Holy" (Isaiah 57:15). "God is light, and in him is no darkness at all" (1 John 1:5). "For I am the Lord your God: ye shall therefore sanctify yourselves, and ye shall be holy; for I am holy" (Leviticus 11:44). "And one cried unto another, and said, Holy, holy,

holy, is the Lord of hosts: the whole earth is full of his glory" (Isaiah 6:3). "Exalt the Lord our God, and worship at his holy hill; for the Lord our God is holy" (Psalm 99:9). "Ye cannot serve the Lord: for he is an holy God" (Joshua 24:19). "Whom hast thou reproached and blasphemed? and against whom hast thou exalted thy voice, and lifted up thine eyes on high? even against the Holy One of Israel" (2 Kings 19:22). "I will also praise thee with the psaltery, even thy truth, O my God: unto thee will I sing with the harp, O thou Holy One of Israel" (Psalm 71:22). "Holy, holy, holy, Lord God Almighty, which was, and is, and is to come" (Revelation 4:8).

The blinding contrast between God and mankind, between holiness and unholiness, is seen in the human reaction whenever God has manifested Himself to humans. In every case, even in the case of "holy" men—unholiness can't bear holiness. When the Lord appeared to Moses in the burning bush, Moses "hid his face; for he was afraid to look upon God" (Exodus 3:6). Job, after glimpsing the Lord, cried out, "I have heard of thee by the hearing of the ear: but now mine eye seeth thee. Wherefore I abhor myself, and repent in dust and ashes" (Job 42:5, 6). Isaiah, after a vision of God sitting upon a throne and being worshiped by angels that sang of His holiness, cried, "Woe is me! for I am undone; because I am a man of unclean lips, and I dwell in the midst of a people of unclean lips: for mine eyes have seen the King, the Lord of hosts" (Isaiah 6:5). Ezekiel, Paul, and John, each in their own way, in their own unique circumstances, got a glimpse of God, and their reactions were always the same—they fell prostrate before Him, unable to bear the sight.

"If the curtain," wrote John R. W. Stott, "which veils the unspeakable majesty of God could be drawn aside but for a moment, we too would not be able to bear the sight. As it were, we only dimly perceive how pure and brilliant must be the glory of almighty God. However, we know enough to realize that sinful man while still in his sins can never approach this holy God. A great chasm yawns between God in His righteousness and man in his sin."[2]

It was, therefore, to bridge this infinite chasm that Christ came. Sin, in a sense, created a new reality, a new dimension, one separated from a holy God. Scientists have speculated on the possibility of other dimensions that can be accessed only through "wormholes," tunnels (possibly behind black holes) that link one universe or dimension with another one. In a sense, Christ functioned like a wormhole; through His life and death, He bridged that infinite gap between God and man. And He could do that *only because He was both God and man.*

Stairway to heaven

Here's why any theology that denies the divinity of Christ (or, for that manner, His humanity) presents a Jesus who cannot save us. Only a being who had been fully "in both camps," only one who is both God and man could bridge the gap between God and man.

There are just two types of existence, created and uncreated. A created being (no matter how exalted) who became a man would simply be shedding one manifestation of creation for another. You can shuffle the cards in the deck endlessly, but you'll always have *only* cards in your hand, never a card-player. A created being could not link us to God the way Christ did, because a created being is still only that—a created being (like rocks, nebulae, and daffodils), *not* the Creator—and a difference as great as that between finitude and infinity exists between the two. If Christ were not God, the bridge, the stairway, might touch earth, but would not reach heaven; if He were not man, it might touch heaven, but not earth. Because Jesus was fully God and fully man, both ends—heaven and earth—are united through Him.

The words of Jesus in John 8:58, "Verily, verily, I say unto you, Before Abraham was, I am"—hinted at His words to Moses centuries earlier, "I AM THAT I AM" (Exodus 3:14). In John's Gospel, Jesus refers to Himself as Deity, a reference not lost on the religious leaders of His day (John 8:59).

"In the beginning was the Word, and the Word was with God, and the Word was God. The same was in the beginning with God. All things were made by him; and without him was not any thing made that was made" (John 1:1-3). If nothing that was made was made without Christ, then He Himself couldn't have been made, because how could He be involved in making Himself if, prior His own existence, He didn't exist and nothing, including Himself, was made without Him? If *all things* made were made by Him—then, logically, He could not have been made, because something that's nonexistent can't make itself.

"For by him were all things created, that are in heaven, and that are in earth, visible and invisible, whether they be thrones, or dominions, or principalities, or powers: all things were created by him, and for him: And he is before all things, and by him all things consist" (Colossians 1:16). Again, if all created things exist through Christ, He Himself could not have been created; if He were, then all things were, in fact, *not* created by Him, contrary to the text. Also, how could He be "before all things" if He were a created being? Something would have to be before Him, which isn't so (according to the text).

Thus, if Jesus Himself were uncreated (which He was), and if through Him all that's created exists (which it does)—then, clearly, Christ has to be God, for who else but God (at least as we understand Him) is the uncreated Creator of all that's created?

But Christ was also a man, and for the same reasons that any theology that downplays or denies Christ's divinity presents a Christ that can't save us, likewise, any theology that downplays or denies His humanity does the same, particularly in light of the clear biblical evidence about His humanity.

"The Word *became flesh* and dwelt among us" (John 1:14, emphasis added), that is, the Word became *human* flesh; He "was born of the seed of David according to the flesh" (Romans 1:3). The Bible says that Jesus was the "Son of Mary" (Mark 6:3) and that He lived through the human stages of life, starting as an infant (Luke 2:7), going through childhood (Luke 2:40, 52), and suffering death (John 19:30, 34). He even referred to Himself (dozens of times) as "the Son of man." According to Scripture, He was "in all things . . . made like unto his brethren" (Hebrews 2:17). He even referred to Himself as a man: "You seek to kill me, a man that hath told you the truth which I have heard of God" (John 8:40). And John had harsh words for those who denied His humanity: "For many deceivers are entered into the world, who confess not that Jesus Christ is come in the flesh" (2 John 1:7).

For centuries there have been endless debates, often fruitless, about the human nature of Christ. Whatever the specifics, such as whether He had the nature of Adam before or after the Fall, one thing remains certain and crucial—Jesus Christ *was human.* He had to be, because only then could the bridge that began in heaven reach all the way down to the earth. Only through Christ's humanity and His divinity could the chasm between the human and the divine be rectified.

"The highest angel in heaven," wrote Ellen White, "had not the power to pay the ransom for one lost soul. Cherubim and seraphim have only the glory with which they are endowed by the Creator as his creatures, and the reconciliation of man to God could be accomplished only through a mediator who was equal with God, possessed of attributes that would dignify, and declare him worthy to treat with the Infinite God in man's behalf, and also represent God to a fallen world. Man's substitute and surety must have man's nature, a connection with the human family whom he was to represent, and, as God's ambassador, he must partake of the divine nature, have a connection with the Infinite, in order to manifest God to the world, and be a mediator between God and man."[3]

"The plan of salvation was opened to Jacob's mind in his dream of a ladder reaching from earth to heaven. Christ was the ladder that he saw. Christ is the link that binds earth to heaven and connects finite man with the infinite God. This ladder reaches from the lowest degradation of earth and humanity to the highest heavens."[4]

"The divine Son of God was the only sacrifice of sufficient value to satisfy the claims of God's perfect law. The angels were sinless, but of less value than the law of God. They were amenable to law. They were messengers to do the will of Christ, and before him to bow. They were created beings, and probationers. Upon Christ no requirements were laid, as upon created beings. He had power to lay down his life, and to take it again. No obligation was laid upon him to undertake the work of atonement. It was a voluntary sacrifice that he made. His life was of sufficient value to rescue man from his fallen condition. The Son of God was in the form of God, and he thought it not robbery to be equal with God. He was the only one, who as a man walked the earth, who could say to all men, Who of you convinceth me of sin? He had united with the Father in the creation of man, and he had power through his own divine perfection of character to atone for man's sin, and to elevate him, and bring him back to his first estate."[5]

The reconciliation

Through sin, humanity severed itself from God; Jesus, as both God and Man, repaired the divide. It's what the Bible calls "the reconciliation"—*the* reconciliation between a perfectly holy God and imperfect, unholy creatures . . . and it happened at the Cross.

"But God commendeth his love toward us, in that, while we were yet sinners, Christ died for us. Much more then, being now justified by his blood, we shall be saved from wrath through him. *"For if, when we were enemies, we were reconciled to God by the death of his Son, much more, being reconciled, we shall be saved by his life."* (Romans 5:8-11, emphasis supplied).

"And all things are of God, *who hath reconciled us to himself by Jesus Christ,* and hath given to us the ministry of reconciliation; To wit, that *God was in Christ, reconciling the world unto himself, not imputing their trespasses unto them;* and hath committed unto us the word of reconciliation. Now then we are ambassadors for Christ, as though God did beseech you by us: we pray you in Christ's stead, *be ye reconciled to God"* (2 Corinthians 5:18-20, emphasis supplied).

"For it pleased the Father that in him should all fulness dwell; And, having made peace through the blood of his cross, by him *to reconcile all things unto himself;* by him, I say, whether they be things in earth, or things in heaven. And you, that were sometime alienated and enemies in your mind by wicked works, *yet now hath he recon-*

ciled in the body of his flesh through death, to present you holy and unblameable and unreproveable in his sight" (Colossians 1:19-22, emphasis supplied).

"For verily he took not on him the nature of angels; but he took on him the seed of Abraham. Wherefore in all things it behoved him to be made like unto his brethren, that he might be a merciful and faithful high priest in things pertaining to God, *to make reconciliation for the sins of the people.* For in that he himself hath suffered being tempted, he is able to succour them that are tempted" (Hebrews 2:16-18, emphasis supplied).

However flat the type may appear on the page, a precipice of truth lies behind these words. Because of sin, we were alienated from our Creator; we were, in fact, His "enemies." But God—by the "death of his son," by the "body of his [Christ's] flesh through death"—*reconciled all things to himself.* What does this mean? Because our sins have, in a sense, offended Him, (or even worse, *estranged* Him from us) God had to reconcile the world unto Himself. He took the initiative to fix the problem that we ourselves created. Though God loved the world after sin—indeed—*because* He loved the world after sin, He had to change its status before Him; otherwise, the entire world would be lost. Though, no doubt, Christ's death on the cross could, and should, affect our attitude about God, the estrangement between heaven and earth was too deep, too cavernous, too rabid to be rectified merely by an attitude adjustment on our part. A change in us, or in how we viewed God, could no more heal the rupture caused by sin than a murderer's sorrow for his crime could resurrect the corpse he created out of living, breathing flesh. Something had to happen to the human race in order for God to accept it, to be reconciled to it, after it sinned against Him. And because there was nothing we could do to bring about that change—God had to do it Himself, which He did, through Christ at Calvary.

In many ways, the verses that encapsulate the crucial idea for understanding this reconciliation are found in Philippians 2:5-8, which reads: "Let this mind be in you, which was also in Christ Jesus: Who, being in the form of God, thought it not robbery to be equal with

God: But made himself of no reputation, and took upon him the form of a servant, and was made in the likeness of men: And being found in fashion as a man, he humbled himself, and became obedient unto death, even the death of the cross." In the RSV, these verses read: "Have this mind among yourselves, which is yours in Christ Jesus, who, though he was in the form of God, did not count equality with God a thing to be grasped, but emptied himself, taking the form of a servant, being born in the likeness of men. And being found in human form he humbled himself and became obedient unto death, even death on a cross." The NIV puts it this way: "Your attitude should be the same as that of Jesus Christ: Who, being in very nature God, did not consider equality with God something to be grasped, but made himself nothing, taking the very nature of a servant, being made in human likeness. And being found in appearance as a man, he humbled himself, and became obedient to death—even death on a cross!"

Here, both Christ's divinity and humanity are revealed; here, the bridge between heaven and earth appears in one picture; here, the contrast between the One "equal with God" who became "as a man" is presented.

But the picture doesn't stop here. It can't, because the rift between the divine and the human needed more than just someone who was both divine and human. Jesus, merely by taking on a human body and coming to our world, could *not* have fixed the rift caused by sin. Jesus could have lived as a human, faced all our toils, sweated all our sweat, cringed with all our pain, cried all our tears, overcome where Adam (or all of us) fell, won all the victories that we so readily lose, and then flown away on a cloud of angels back to heaven, having proved that we can, indeed, obey God's law. Yet that wasn't enough to save us, wasn't enough to reconcile the world to God; if it was, His mission would have ended before the trauma and passion of the Cross. If anything, Christ's having lived a perfect life without the Cross would have made the problem worse, because by His life Christ proved that disobedience isn't necessary, which would have only heightened the gravity of Adam's (and our) sin. More was needed to save us, and Philippians says what that was: God, as a human, had to die—"even the death of the cross."

The two substitutions

Why? This question gets to the essence of biblical Christianity, the crucial pivot point of faith, the place from which we must begin—*substitution,* the foundation of the reconciliation. Without it, Adam and Eve would have immediately become fertilizer for some of Eden's flowers, you wouldn't be reading these words, and the world could have ended almost as soon as it began. To avoid these consequences, the Lord—in His unfathomable graciousness—made a provision, even before humanity sinned (Rev 13:8), that would allow the fallen race to be restored. This restoration would come, not because of anything a sinner could do (sin was too serious a problem for the guilty party to rectify), but because God provided a *Substitute* who would take the place of the fallen race. Rather than throwing out the defective parts (as one might replace a defective tire), God provided a Substitute who became our Representative instead, Someone who possessed none of the baggage that caused us to be condemned to begin with.

In Romans 5, Paul states how we fell and then how we are saved from that fall: "(For if through the offense of one many be dead, much more the grace of God, and the gift by grace, which is by one man, Jesus Christ, hath abounded unto many. And not as it was by one that sinned, so is the gift: for the judgment was by one to condemnation, but the free gift is of many offenses unto justification. For if by one man's offense death reigned by one; much more they which receive abundance of grace and of the gift of righteousness shall reign in life by one, Jesus Christ.) Therefore as by the offense of one judgment came upon all men to condemnation; even so by the righteousness of one the free gift came upon all men unto justification of life. For as by one man's disobedience many were made sinners, so by the obedience of one shall many be made righteous" (Romans 5:15-19).

Through Adam's offense "judgment came upon all men to condemnation," which meant everyone faced inevitable and unavoidable doom. Through Christ, however, the inevitable became evitable, and the doom avoidable. When Adam fell, the world *as a whole* was condemned; through Christ's *substitutionary* life and *substitutionary* death, the world *as a whole* was given a second chance, a reprieve, an opportunity to avert the condemnation that Adam, our first father, brought upon all. Whatever Adam did to the race *as a whole* through "disobedience," Christ came to undo *as a whole* through "obedience"—even unto death.

Scripture has subsumed humanity under two representatives—Adam and Christ. Our corporate fate has, by default, placed us all under Adam, through whom sin entered the world, which means everyone who was, is, or will be (except One) was, is, or will be sinners. We have no choice in this fate anymore than we can choose our birth parents; sin is as much a part of human nature as is breath, and that nature ceases only when the breath does: "Through one man sin entered the world, and death through sin, and thus death spread to all men" (Romans 5:12).

But Christ, "the last Adam" (1 Corinthians 15:45), offers each the opportunity to be represented by Him, as opposed to the first Adam. It's what the Bible calls "adoption" (Ephesians 1:5). Jesus, as the Last Adam (sometimes called the Second Adam), became a human and covered the same ground that the first Adam, our natural father, did. The difference, however, is that Jesus succeeded where Adam failed, and the incredible provision of the gospel is that the Lord will accept Christ's success in place of Adam's failure. Just as Adam's sin brought all to death, Christ's success gives all life because He becomes the new Representative of all who choose Him. "For as by one man's disobedience many were made sinners, so by the obedience of one shall many be made righteous" (Romans 5:19).

This concept of a new Representative, a Second Adam, forms the essence of substitution—and the reconciliation. God accepts Christ's success in place of Adam's failure. As a result, those who accept that substitution, who choose to place themselves under the Second Adam, have His success counted as their own, thus reconciling them to God. Without that substitution, that change of representation, we are all dead in our sins, and our lives and all we will ever be, or do, or could hope for, will be consummated, completed, and capped in the grave.

"For if by one man's offense death reigned by one; much more they which receive abundance of grace and of the gift of righteousness shall reign in life by one, Jesus Christ" (Romans 5:17).

Just as the failure of the race's first representative brought humanity into disrepute, the success of the Last Representative gave humanity a new status, a new start, before the Father, in that the condemnation of sin was no longer an absolute surety. The death that was to come to everyone didn't have to come to anyone; the doom that Adam's fall brought to each person, individually, could be averted for each person, individually. Everyone, from Adam onward, was given a second chance thanks to the Second Adam.

"We have reason for ceaseless gratitude to God that Christ, by His perfect obedience, has won back the heaven that Adam lost through disobedience. Adam sinned, and the children of Adam share his guilt and its consequences; but Jesus bore the guilt of Adam, and all the children of Adam that will flee to Christ, the second Adam, may escape the penalty of transgression. Jesus regained heaven for man by bearing the test that Adam failed to endure; for He obeyed the law perfectly. . . ."[6]

"Christ, the second Adam, came in the likeness of sinful flesh. In man's behalf, He became subject to sorrow, to weariness, to hunger, and to thirst. He was subject to temptation, but He yielded not to sin. No taint of sin was upon Him. He declared, 'I have kept my Father's commandments [in My earthly life]' (John 15:10). He had infinite power only because He was perfectly obedient to His Father's will. The second Adam stood the test of trial and temptation that He might become the Owner of all humanity."[7]

The great news of the good news, however, doesn't end with the substitutionary aspect of Christ's life, the perfect life that God accepts in place of our imperfect ones, the flawless lawfulness that substitutes for our awful lawlessness. Sin—to be expiated, to be resolved, to be justly eradicated—needed more than just one sinless life to substitute for a world of sinful ones, because a sinless life, in and of itself, couldn't deal with the *penalty* for transgression. Life can't answer sin; only death can—for "without shedding of blood is no remission" of sin (Hebrews 9:22).

If the Jewish sanctuary taught anything, it taught that blood, that death, was needed for atonement. "For the life of the flesh is in the blood: and I have given it to you upon the altar to make an atonement for your souls: for it *is the blood that maketh an atonement for the soul"* (Leviticus 17:11, emphasis supplied). Presenting a spotless lamb before the altar without sacrificing it wouldn't release the sinner from the legal consequences of sin any more than cooking a meal without eating it will fill an empty stomach. Atonement, reconciliation, came *after* death, *after* blood was shed, not before.

That's why Christ's life and death were inseparable components of salvation. His life is what gave His death its meaning and, most importantly, its saving efficacy. Without His life, His death would have meant nothing, at least in terms of salvation (and, as far as we are concerned, without salvation, what do we have?). Just as His life, of itself, couldn't atone for sin—His death, of itself, couldn't either. That death, to be efficacious, to atone for sin, needed the perfect life that preceded it; otherwise, that death would have been inadequate. If Christ had sinned, neither His life nor His death could have saved Mother Teresa, much less any of us. A sinner dying for other sinners leads only to more death, never to eternal life.

Thus Philippians 5:2-8 didn't end with the One who, though equal with God, became a servant—because His becoming a servant, of itself, was not enough to save. The verses end with His death, because without the death, His servanthood would have been a nice gesture on God's part, but our human condition is too degenerate, too desperate, for a nice gesture to save us.

Thus, two aspects of substitution—a substitutionary life and a substitutionary death—formed the foundation of the reconciliation. First, redemption, reconciliation, demanded a life of perfect obedience, a life that fulfilled all the demands of the law for everyone. Secondly, redemption demanded death as the full punishment for every sin of every sinner. A just and righteous God had to punish all sin, but in His mercy He punished them in the person of Jesus, the only Person who didn't deserve punishment because He was the only Person who never sinned.

"But we see Jesus, who was made a little lower than the angels for the suffering of death, crowned with glory and honour; that he by the grace of God *should taste death for every man"* (Hebrews 2:9, emphasis supplied), that's death for *every* human being, even the worst the species has produced. From Cain to Joseph Mengele, from the homosexual rapists in Sodom to the pornographers in California, from the person who stuck a spear in Christ's side to the one who lit the fire that burned John Huss, from Adam's first sin to the last man's last sin *and every one in between*—the legal penalty for the most outrageous and sadistic and lustful deeds has been paid, in full, by Jesus at the Cross. No one's sin, no matter how wretched, inconceivable, or utterly inexcusable, was missed at the Cross, which means that no one, no matter how wretched or inconceivably inexcusable, would need to face God's punishment for their wretchedly inconceivable and inexcusable deeds.

Hard as it is for narrow Euclidian and unforgiving minds to grasp, Jesus bore the righteous judgment of a righteous God against all sin, with not one transgression—from the Rape of Nanking to King David's most lustful thoughts—left out or unpaid for. No sin could have been overlooked, for if even one sin had been missed, then the person who had committed it would have no chance of salvation. And that's impossible because Christ died for everyone; and for that death to save anyone, all sin had to be paid for, no exceptions allowed. "No sin," wrote Ellen White, "can be committed by man for which satisfaction has not been met on Calvary."[8] To borrow an analogy from accounting, the books had to be perfectly balanced, down to the penny.

"And he is the propitiation for our sins: and not for ours only, but also for *the sins of the whole world"* (1 John 2:2, emphasis supplied). "Now we believe, not because of thy saying: for we have heard him ourselves and know that this is indeed the Christ, the *Saviour of the world"* (John 4:42, emphasis supplied). "We have seen and do testify that the Father has sent the Son to be *the Saviour of the world"* (1 John 4:14, emphasis supplied). "For God so loved *the world* . . . ." (John 3:16, emphasis supplied). "We trust in the living God, who is the Saviour *of all men,* specially of those that believe" (1 Timothy 4:10, empahsis supplied).

If no one can be saved unless all his sins were paid for, and if Christ died to save every person—then He, obviously, must have paid for every person's every sin, which He did: "The atonement for a lost world," wrote Ellen White, "was to be full, abundant, and complete. Christ's offering was exceedingly abundant, reaching every soul that God had created."[9] Jesus, as the second Adam—through His perfect life and atoning death—put *the whole world,* everyone, in a new position before the Father, one that offers everyone the *opportunity* to be spared the condemnation that sin brings.

"For if by one man's offense death reigned by one; much more *they which receive abundance of grace* and of the gift of righteousness shall reign in life by one, Jesus Christ" (Romans 5:17, emphasis supplied). Here is where all humanity divides into two camps—those who receive "abundance of grace and of the gift of righteousness" and those who don't. In contrast, all other divisions—gender, race, economics, politics, religion—fade into puerile obsolescence. To be on the wrong side here means, ultimately, eternal death—the unfortunate denouement for untold multitudes, because however complete, universal, and all-encompassing Christ's substitution, many will choose not to reap the ultimate benefit from it.

If Christ's death gave everyone a second chance at eternal life, but not everyone will receive this life, the decisive, personal factor, then, must be the *individual* human response. Otherwise, Christ's death would have meant unconditional, universal salvation, which it didn't. That a person will not be saved from an act done specifically to save him reveals that his personal response to this act is the crucial, determining variable. How else can one explain the phenomenon of souls engulfed in the lake of fire when Christ's death encompassed everyone, even those who do, eventually, burn.

The important question is: How do *individuals* respond to this second chance, this reprieve, this opportunity that Christ has provided? It gets to the core of the Protestant-Catholic divide. Here is where Protestants and Catholics—no matter how much they co-opt each other's symbols and language—exist in radically different theological universes. Both faiths have opposite understandings, not only of what that response entails, but of the question itself—How are we saved? And unless one side sells its soul on fundamental issues, these intractable opposites will remain, even if covered up by blurry-worded documents to the contrary.

"Alien righteousness"

So far this chapter has established: that because of sin, an infinite chasm separated God and humanity; that Christ, as both God and human, bridged that chasm; that His life met all the demands of God's law, His death all the demands of God's justice; that with both demands met, fallen humanity now stood in a different relationship to God; and that because of Jesus, the world was given a second chance at the eternal life, which was originally forfeited through Adam. However, because the provision for eternal life must be accepted individually—a crucial question remains: How does a person, *individually,* reap the ultimate benefits of what Christ has done for the world, corporately?

For Protestants, the answer is easy—those benefits come by faith, and faith *alone.* Considering not just the infinite gap between heaven and earth (and how helpless humans are of themselves to bridge it), but the incredible price it cost to heal that gap, it would mock not only the seriousness of sin, but the cost of redemption from it for salvation to be by anything other than by faith alone. How bad could sin be if, we—pathetic mammals brimming with bile, vile with lust, and lush with covetousness—could do anything to save ourselves from its consequences? Those who think we can somehow work our way out of the problem haven't sufficiently considered the seriousness of sin.

Also, if salvation comes by anything other than by faith, then the fact that God the Son became human flesh, lived a perfect life of obedience to the law, even fulfilled all demands of the law, and then went to the cross where He faced the Father's wrath for sin, where all the world's sin fell upon Him, where He became sin for us, where He was judged and condemned in our place, and where He died the second death as a Substitute for the transgressions of the whole world—*all this still wouldn't be enough to save us!* Something else would be needed to make up for whatever deficiencies remained after the Cross, and that "something else" would be our sin-stained, imperfect law keeping. Please! Could anything be more ludicrous?

Finally, if salvation comes by anything other than by faith, then it's no longer by grace, but by debt. If we could do anything, in any way, no matter how subtly or slightly, to merit salvation, then it becomes owed to us, something we deserve—which, of course, we don't.

"What shall we say then that Abraham our father, as pertaining to the flesh, hath found? For if Abraham were justified by works, he hath whereof to glory; but not before God. For what saith the scripture? Abraham believed God, and it was counted unto him for righteousness. *Now to him that worketh is the reward not reckoned of grace, but of debt.* But to him that worketh not, but believeth on him that justifieth the ungodly, his faith is counted for righteousness" (Romans 4:1-5, emphasis supplied).

If salvation came by works, it would no longer be "reckoned of grace but of debt" (the NAS translates these verses, "his wage is not reckoned as a favor, but as what is due"). A debt is what you are owed or what you are due, and we are definitely not owed or due salvation. That's why salvation has to be by God's grace alone, which comes by faith alone; any other way means it's no longer by grace.

"Let the subject be made distinct and plain," wrote Ellen White, "that it is not possible to effect anything in our standing before God or in the gift of God to us through creature merit. Should faith and works purchase the gift of salvation for anyone, then the Creator is under obligation to the creature. Here is an opportunity for falsehood to be accepted as truth. If any man can merit salvation by anything he may do, then he is in the same position as the Catholic to do penance for his sins. Salvation, then, is partly of debt, that may be earned as wages. If man cannot, by any of his good works, merit salvation, then it must be wholly of grace, received by man as a sinner because he receives and believes in Jesus. It is wholly a free gift. Justification by faith is placed beyond controversy. And all this controversy is ended, as soon as the matter is settled that the merits of fallen man in his good works can never procure eternal life for him."[10]

That salvation isn't procured by good works doesn't mean, however, that good works aren't an essential, inseparable part of the salvation experience. On the contrary. The Bible—particularly the New Testament, particularly the Gospels, particularly the words of Jesus Himself—stress how essential works are in the Christian life. According to Paul, "We are his workmanship, created in Christ Jesus for good works, which God prepared beforehand, that we should walk in them" (Ephesians 2:10, RSV).

We were created for good works, which were foreordained for us to do? Thus, no more than you could have a one-sided coin, neither could you have faith without works, justification without sanctification, or salvation without obedience. One immediately and, of theological necessity, follows the other, To claim justification as something totally separate and alien from sanctification *in the personal experience of the believer* is to try to separate wetness from water.

Justification and sanctification are two different things, of course; they have two different roles, two different meanings. One describes the *means* of salvation and one the *results*. One is legal, forensic, and in a sense outside of us, while the other is subjective, personal, and intrinsic to the Christian. Yet no way do the legal means of salvation somehow preclude, or exclude, the subjective personal results, or fruits, of that salvation. More verses in Scripture talk about Christian living, about obedience, about personal holiness, about keeping the law, about overcoming sin, about Christ changing our lives, about reflecting God's love than talk about justification by faith. Jesus spent more time showing people how to live after they had been saved than He did on how to be saved to begin with. Only through a perverted, unbalanced, and dishonest use of the Bible could anyone believe that justification by faith means that how we live has *no* bearing on our relationship with God.

That we're saved by faith, and not by works, doesn't mean that works have nothing to do with saving faith. That we can never trust in our good works for salvation doesn't mean that works don't play a part in the experience of salvation. Works are an outward expression of an inward relationship with our Creator and Redeemer. Works express faith; works are the personification of faith; works are the heart and soul of faith; works are the human manifestation of faith. Works are faith made real, belief made tangible, our words and profession made flesh. Works are a means of expressing, even strengthening, faith—and maybe nothing Jesus said better expressed the role of works in maintaining, expressing, and strengthening faith than this parable:

"Therefore whosoever heareth these sayings of mine, *and doeth them,* I will liken him unto a wise man, which built his house upon a rock: And the rain descended, and the floods came, and the winds blew, and beat upon that house; and it fell not: for it was founded upon a rock. And every one that heareth these sayings of mine, *and doeth them not,* shall be likened unto a foolish man, which built his house upon the sand. And the rain descended, and the floods came, and the winds blew, and beat upon that house; and it fell: and great was the fall of it" (Matthew 7:24-27, emphasis supplied).

One obeyed, one didn't—and that obedience made the difference between building on rock or on sand, the difference between enduring to the end or being swept away. It wasn't the house itself, by anything intrinsic to it, that withstood the storm; it was the foundation upon which it was built that kept it from falling—and that foundation was Christ. The house, in and of itself, no matter how well built, could never stand; its security was found only in the foundation upon which it rested.

Through works faith endures. Though it's too late for works to save us (just as it's too late for a blood transfusion to save a corpse), James showed the inseparable relationship between the faith and works: "By works was faith made perfect" (James 2:22).

At the same time, whatever role works have in the experience of salvation, if salvation can never be procured by our works, and if "it is not possible to effect anything in our standing before God or in the gift of God to us through creature merit," then the righteousness that saves us must be a righteousness *outside of us,* an extrinsic righteousness, what Luther called an "alien righteousness,"[11] what Paul called "the righteousness of God" (Romans 3:22)—the righteousness that Jesus worked out in His life alone and that is credited to us by faith alone.

"Therefore by the deeds of the law there shall no flesh be justified in his sight: for by the law is the knowledge of sin. But now *the righteousness of God without the law is manifested,* being witnessed by the law and the prophets; Even *the righteousness of God* which is by faith of Jesus Christ unto all and upon all them that believe" (Romans 3:20-22, emphasis supplied).

This is a righteousness outside of us, a righteousness that exists millions (maybe billions) of light years away from us, the righteousness of God found in the person of Jesus Christ, our High Priest in heaven, a righteousness that will never fade, never be corrupted, never fail, and never end, a righteousness in no way dependent upon human follies. Wrote John Bunyan: "Indeed, this is one of the greatest mysteries of the world—namely, that a righteousness that resides with a person in heaven should justify me, a sinner, on earth."

Logically, what alternatives exist once we accept the following three premises? If Christ's death was for everyone (which it was), if not everyone is saved (which they're not), and if works cannot save anyone (which they can't)—then how, possibly, can the saved be saved by anything other than by *faith* in a righteousness *outside of them?* If this saving righteousness were in them, then, however subtly, salvation would still have to be by works, by something that these people do because of a righteousness manifested in them that changes them and what they do, a righteousness that expresses itself in good works. How can someone have an intrinsic, personal righteousness working within them that does not change them? They can't, which means that this righteousness, ultimately, is one of their own good works—and that isn't "the righteousness of God" that Paul talks about, the righteousness that gives us a perfect standing before God.

To argue that it's not our works, but God's works in us, is the type of casuistry scribbled into these bogus documents of unity between Protestants and Catholics in order to proclaim a theological unity that exists only in the synaptic clefts of the subjective imagination, and not in objective reality. God doesn't force Himself upon us or into us. He doesn't make us do good works. If some folks do good works, and some don't, it's only because some have made a choice to allow God to work in them in order that they can do these works, and some have made a choice *not* to allow Him. If God, working in Mother Teresa, used her to feed orphans, it's still Mother Teresa feeding orphans, and all the metaphysical, mystical, and theological sophistry to the contrary can't change that fact. It's something in her, something intrinsic to who she is, that results in something that *she* does, something that results in *her* works—and if these works, in any way, make her righteous before God, then she's saved, not by faith alone, but also by works. The claim that these are God's works in us and not our own, only pushes the argument one step backward; it doesn't change the fundamental issue, which is that if salvation is by anything other than a righteousness outside of us, then it is, of necessity, by our works, whether their origin is, or is not, in God.

Again, that's why salvation has to come, not only by a righteousness outside of us, but by faith alone in that righteousness. If it were anything other than by faith, then it would, of necessity, be by works. What other options exist other than faith or works (words are "works," in the sense that they are something we do with our mouths)? The only other option is divine fiat, in which God selects those who are saved and those who are lost totally independent of individual choice, which (amazingly enough) many Christians believe. If salvation is not by faith and not by divine fiat, how else could the saved be saved other than by their works? Yet Scripture is more than clear that salvation can't be by works, because then it's no longer by grace. Therefore, it has to be by faith, and faith alone.

"For therein is the righteousness of God revealed from faith to faith: as it is written, The just shall live by faith" (Romans 1:17).

"Even the righteousness of God which is by faith of Jesus Christ unto all and upon all them that believe: for there is no difference" (Romans 3:22).

"For the promise, that he should be the heir of the world, was not to Abraham, or to his seed, through the law, but through the righteousness of faith" (Romans 4:13).

"For we through the Spirit wait for the hope of righteousness by faith" (Galatians 5:5).

"Noah . . . became heir of the righteousness which is by faith" (Hebrews 11:7).

"But to him that worketh not, but believeth on him that justifieth the ungodly, his faith is counted for righteousness" (Romans 4:5).

"What shall we say then? That the Gentiles, which followed not after righteousness, have attained to righteousness, even the righteousness which is of faith" (Romans 9:30).

"Every soul may say: 'By His perfect obedience He has satisfied the claims of the law, and my only hope is found in looking to Him as my substitute and surety, who obeyed the law perfectly for me. By faith in His merits I am free from the condemnation of the law. He clothes me with His righteousness, which answers all the demands of the law. I am complete in Him who brings in everlasting righteousness. He presents me to God in the spotless garment of which no thread was woven by any human agent.' "[12]

Here, in these words, is the essence of Protestantism, the essence of the Reformation, the essence of the doctrine of justification by faith alone. The "spotless garment of which no thread was woven by any human agent" is "the righteousness of God," the righteousness that comes by faith, the righteousness that saves us, a righteousness that exists outside of us *(extra nos)*—the only righteousness by which we can be made right with God. In this righteousness, which we acquire by faith, the question, *How are we saved?* finds its only answer.

What, then, are the "finest standards" of Protestantism? They can be sharpened down, polished, and hewn into two clear and cutting points that can't be compromised, even slightly, without ruining them any more than one can tweak, modify, or compromise the sum of 2 + 2. First, we are saved by a righteousness outside of us; second, this righteousness is credited to us by faith, and faith alone. These two points are nonnegotiable; their nature allows for no concessions, no compromise. Either it's a righteousness totally outside of us, or it is not; either it is by faith alone, or it is not. There's no middle ground, nor can there ever be.

And, as the rest of this book will show, to try to meld the Protestant understanding of justification with the Roman isn't merely trying to bring together a positive and negative electric charge that are doing nothing more than repelling each other. Instead, trying to meld Roman and Protestant theology on justification is like trying to bring together matter and antimatter: they meet—and destroy each other.

---

1. *Canons and Decrees of the Council of Trent.* Rev. H.J. Schroeder, O.P. (Rockford, Ill.:Tan Books) Canon 9. p. 43.
2. John Stott. *Basic Christianity* (Grand Rapids, Mich.: Eerdmans) 1966, pp. 73, 74.
3. *Advent Review and Sabbath Herald.* 12-22-1891.
4. *Apples of Gold Library* 08-01-98.
5. *Second Advent Review and Sabbath Herald,* 12-17-1872.
6. *Faith and Works,* pp. 88, 89.
7. *Selected Messages,* vol. 3, p. 142.
8. 1SM, p. 343.
9. YI July 19, 1900.
10. *Faith and Works,* pp.19, 20.
11. Martin Luther. *What Luther Says: An Anthology*. Ed. Edwald M. Plass (St. Louis: Concordia) 1959, 2:711.
12. 1SM, p. 396.

CHAPTER FIVE

Let Him Be Anathema

Frank McCourt, in his best selling memoir *Angela's Ashes,* tells about his baptism as an infant. Frank's father, drunk and angry at the presiding priest, threatened to beat up the cleric just as the ritual began. McCourt recounts what followed:

"Angela, new mother, agitated, forgot she was holding the child and let him slip into the baptismal font, a total immersion of the Protestant type. The altar boy assisting the priest plucked the infant from the font and restored him to Angela, who sobbed and clutched him, dripping. The priest laughed, said he had never seen the like, that the child was a regular little Baptist now and hardly needed a priest."[1]

However cute, this anecdote contains an element that exposes the impossible, and hopelessly impassable, Protestant-Catholic divide. Baby Frank, totally immersed, "was a regular little Baptist now and hardly needed a priest." Baby Frank, of course, and everyone else, *never* needs a priest, a least the human one to which this cleric referred. Jesus is our High Priest, and He ministers in heaven the merits of His once-and-for-all efficacious sacrifice in our behalf. "For

Christ is not entered into the holy places made with hands, which are the figures of the true; but into heaven itself, now to appear in the presence of God for us: Nor yet that he should offer himself often, as the high priest entereth into the holy place every year with blood of others; For then must he often have suffered since the foundation of the world: but now once in the end of the world hath he appeared to put away sin by the sacrifice of himself" (Hebrews 9:24-26).

McCourt's corny tale touches, peripherally, the fundamental differences that make Protestantism and Catholicism incompatible, even contradictory, religions, no matter the common linguistic trappings ceremoniously draped over both. There are three of these differences, none of which, by its essence, allows for compromise.

The first difference deals with *saving* grace: Is it infused in us or does it remain outside the believer? The second deals with how that grace is obtained: By faith alone, or is something else needed? The third deals with what is really the core of the matter—ecclesiology: Does one need a church to mediate God's saving grace to the sinner?

Responding to Mark Noll's amazing statement that neither Protestants or Catholics should convert those who hold to the "the finest standards of either faith," we looked in chapter 4 at "the finest standards" of Protestantism on the question: *How are we saved?* This present chapter examines "the finest standards" of Catholicism on the same question, but seeks to answer another one as well: *Does any ground of unity exist between Protestants and Catholic on the question of salvation or are the differences so vast and impenetrable that none can be bridged without one side changing fundamentals so essential to its identity that to change would be to compromise, or even to lose, that identity?*

Gratia infusia

Contrary to popular misconceptions, Rome teaches not only that we're saved by grace, but that we're saved by grace *alone*. Even at Trent, where Rome spent eighteen years formulating its response to the Protestant revolt, justification by grace was affirmed. Canon 1 (of the sixth session) states: "If anyone says that man can be justified before God by his own works, whether done by his own natural powers or through the teaching of the law, without divine grace through Jesus, let him be anathema."[2] More than 400 years later, in the new *Catechism of the Catholic Church,* Rome reiterated this position: "Our justification comes from the grace of God. Grace is *favor*, the *free and undeserved help* that God gives us to respond to his call to become children of God."[3]

The problem, therefore, isn't whether justification is by grace, or even by grace alone; most Catholics would agree with both statements. Instead, the question that must be addressed is: *What does one mean by the word "grace," especially in the context of justification?* Here's the crux of the matter. For Rome, justifying grace is something that happens, not just outside of us (as Protestants teach), but *within us* as well—a crucial difference that has kept, and must forever keep, Protestants and Catholics as divided theologically as are Jews and Christians over belief in, or rejection of, Jesus as Messiah.

Despite the linguistic gerrymandering and theological camouflage of documents like *The Gift of Salvation, Evangelicals and Catholics Together* and the *Joint Declaration on the Doctrine of Justification,* Rome is unequivocal when speaking to her own regarding justification—without the language games that so successfully placate naive Protestants. Whatever the legal or forensic elements involved in justification (which Rome doesn't deny), justification includes *a process within* a person—a process that *changes* a person, a process that not only declares a person righteous, but *makes* that person righteous. This belief is so fundamental to Catholic theology that to give it up would be ecclesiastical suicide for reasons that will become apparent later, something that Rome—after surviving more than 1,400 years—isn't about to do.

At the Council of Trent, Rome staked out its position on justification and hasn't budged on it since, no matter how much men such as Pat Robertson and Charles Colson want Protestants to believe differently.

Said the Council of Trent regarding justification: "This disposition or preparation is followed by justification itself, *which is not only a remission of sins but also the sanctification and renewal of the inward man through the voluntary reception of the grace and gifts whereby an unjust man becomes just . . .* by that which He makes us just, that, namely, with which we being endowed by Him, are renewed in the spirit of our mind, *and not only are we reputed, but we are truly called and are just, receiving justice* [righteousness] *within us,* each according to his own measure, which the Holy Ghost distributes to everyone as He will, and according to each one's disposition and cooperation. For though no one can be just except he to whom the merits of the passion of our Lord Jesus Christ are communicated, yet this takes place in that justification of the sinner, *when by the merit of the most holy passion, the charity of God is poured forth by the Holy Ghost in the hearts of those who are justified and inheres in them;* whence man through Jesus Christ, in whom He is engrafted, *receives in that justification, together with the remission of sins, all these infused at the same time, namely, faith, hope, and charity"* (italics supplied).[4]

"Thus, neither is our own justice [righteousness] established as from ourselves, nor is the justice [righteousness] of God ignored or repudiated, for that justice, which is called ours, because we *are justified by its inherence in us,* that same is of God, because *it is infused in us* by God through the merit of Christ" (italics supplied).[5]

"If anyone says that men are justified either by the sole imputation of the justice [righteousness] of Christ or by the sole remission of sins, *to the exclusion of the grace and the charity which is poured forth in their hearts by the Holy Ghost,* and remains in them, or also that the grace by which we are justified is only the good will of God, let him be anathema" (italics supplied).[6]

"If anyone says that justifying grace is nothing else than confidence [faith] in divine mercy, which remits sins for Christ's sake, or that it is this confidence [faith] alone that justifies us, let him be anathema."[7]

"If anyone says that the justice [righteousness] received is not preserved and also not increased before God through good works, but that those good works are merely the fruits and signs of justification obtained, but not the cause of its increase, let him be anathema."[8]

"If anyone says that after the reception of the grace of justification the guilt is so remitted and the debt of eternal punishment so blotted out *that no debt or temporal punishment remains to be discharged either in this world or in purgatory before the gates of heaven can be opened,* let him be anathema" (italics supplied).[9]

"If anyone says that the good works of the one justified are in such manner the gifts of God that they are also not the good merits of him justified; *or that the one justified by the good works that he performs by the grace of God* and the merit of Jesus Christ, whose living member he is, does not truly merit an increase in grace, eternal life, and in case he dies in grace, the attainment of eternal life itself and also an increase in glory, let him be anathema" (italics supplied).[10]

Of course, the Council of Trent took place in the 1500s; a lot has changed since then. But a lot hasn't, either, including Rome's view of justification as expressed by the Council. In fact, *The Catechism of the Catholic Church*—which represents the "finest standards" of Roman Catholic theology—reiterates the Tridentine position.

"Justification," says the catechism, "is not only the remission of sins, *but also the sanctification and renewal of the interior man"* (italics supplied).[11]

"The grace of the Holy Spirit," continues the *Catechism,* "has the power to justify us, that is, to cleanse us from our sins and to communicate to us 'the righteousness of God through faith in Jesus Christ' and through Baptism. "[12]

"The Holy Spirit is the master of the interior life. By giving birth to the 'inner man,' justification entails the *sanctification* of his whole being" (italics in original).[13]

"The merit of man before God in the Christian life arises from the fact that God *has freely chosen to associate man with the work of his grace.* The fatherly action of God is first on his own initiative, and then follows man's free acting through his collaboration, so that the merit of good works is to be attributed in the first place to the grace of God, then to the faithful" (italics in original, underlining supplied).[14]

"No one can merit the initial grace which is at the origin of conversion. Moved by the Holy Spirit, *we can merit for ourselves and for others all the graces needed to attain eternal life"* (italics supplied).[15]

"Justification includes the remission of sins, sanctification, and the renewal of the inner man."[16]

Whatever theological tweaking has taken place over the centuries, Rome hasn't deviated on its position that justification by faith, though coming only from God's grace, is not limited to an extrinsic remission of sins or to a mere declaration of righteousness—but, instead (to use the words of Trent and the catechism) is also "the sanctification and renewal of the inner man."[17]

This point contains the pivot upon which Western Christianity split, upon which the Reformation fires were first stoked, upon which Protestantism was founded, and upon which the religion of Christ is distinguished from the religion of antichrist. Most of the other issues that separate Catholicism from Protestantism—purgatory, indulgences, the Mass, penance, and the priesthood—originate in one degree or another from the Roman notion that justification includes a righteousness that is infused into the life of the believer, as opposed to the Protestant teaching that justification is the imputation of God's righteousness, nothing more.

The *Catechism Of the Catholic Church,* unlike Trent, didn't hurl anathemas upon those who believed that "good works are merely the fruits and signs of justification obtained, but not the cause of its increase"[18] (which is, by the way, a fundamental tenet of justification by faith alone and one of "the finest standards" of Protestantism). However, the *Catechism* was unequivocal about justification being more than a legal declaration. The *Catechism* reiterates, one way or another, the crucial Roman teaching that justification includes a process that occurs within a believer. "Justification includes," it says, "the *remission of sins, sanctification,* and the *renewal of the inner man"* (italics supplied).

This point can't be overemphasized. Despite all the loving pronouncements of unity between Catholics and Protestants on justification by faith, the catechism proves that Rome holds the same view of justification by faith that it did more than four hundred years ago—a view that ignited the Reformation, a view that perhaps more than any other convinced the Reformers (and rightly so) that Rome was the antichrist warned about by Daniel, Paul, and John.

But doesn't Protestantism teach that God's grace works an inner renewal in the heart of a Christian? Don't Protestants teach that God's grace makes a person righteous? Doesn't the Bible teach that the Holy Spirit works within a Christian to give him faith, hope, and charity? Why this strong antipathy against the notion of God working within a believer? Doesn't the Bible talk about Christ working in us, to change us, so that we can perform good works and be conformed into His likeness? Isn't holy living essential to Christianity? Doesn't the Bible teach that we should all live faithful, even blameless, lives through the power of Christ working in us?

Of course it does! No serious, balanced Protestant claims otherwise. The issue has not, nor has ever, been (at least within mainstream Protestantism) about the biblical promises that God's grace will bring an inner renewal, an inner change, within a Christian. Almost all Protestants agree that God's grace does bring that inner change and that one can't be a true Christian without this change.

The question, instead, is this: What role does this "renewal of the inner man . . . sanctification . . . the cleansing of sin . . . the receiving of righteousness within us" play in our legal standing with God? Or, to ask it more simply: *How are we saved?* Is it by the renewal of the inner man, the cleansing of sin within us, and sanctification? Or are we saved, justified, only by the righteousness that exists in Jesus Himself and in the life He lived as our Substitute—and never by any righteousness in ourselves, no matter how much inner renewal, sanctification, and holiness through the power of the Spirit does happen within us?

Protestants don't deny the inner work of the Spirit in the life of the believer. What they do deny, and must always deny, is that our standing with God, our acceptance with God, our justification, is based on this inner renewal or that this inner renewal and good works are a means by which our justification is "increased before God." That justification and sanctification are both part of the Christian experience, in fact inseparable parts, almost all Protestants would accept. But justification and sanctification have two distinct functions that cannot be melded.

Immediately after Trent ended, Protestant apologist Martin Chemnitz wrote a massive text called *Examination of the Council of Trent,* which took issue with the council on (among other things) the meaning of justification by faith.

"We do not," wrote Chemnitz, "for this reason confuse them [justification and sanctification] but rather distinguish them, so that we may assign to each its place, order, and peculiar nature, as we have learned from Scripture, namely, so that reconciliation, or remission of sins, precedes, and the beginning of love, or of the new obedience, follow after; chiefly, however, that faith may be certain that has a reconciled God and remission of sins not because of the renewal, which follows and which has been begun, but because of the Mediator, the Son of God."[19]

Wrote Chemnitz again: "What the conscience should set up as the thing on account of which the adoption may be bestowed upon us, on what confidence can be safely reposed that we shall be accepted to eternal life, etc.; whether it is the satisfaction, obedience, and the merit of the Son of God, the Mediator, or, indeed, the renewal which has begun in us, the love, and the other virtues in us. Here is the point at issue in the controversy, which is so studiously and deceitfully concealed."[20]

And again: "This is not the point in dispute, whether the renewal belongs to the benefits of Christ, whether a person, when he is reconciled to God, is at the same time also renewed through the Holy Spirit, whether the new obedience ought to follow. For these things we teach plainly and clearly. But this is the question, how and why can we be justified, so that we may be received by God into grace and be accepted to eternal life? These things must be repeated so often lest they misrepresent this dispute concerning the meaning of the word 'justify,' as if we denied the renewal in its proper place and order."[21]

If, however, Protestants and Catholics agree that inner renewal is a part of the overall Christian experience, what difference does it make whether or not the phrase "inner renewal" is included under the title of "justification"? Everyone agrees that inner renewal happens; isn't that enough? If, after all, both churches believe in inner renewal, then isn't the battle merely over semantics, over (as Chemnitz said) "the meaning of the word 'justify' "? Why divide Christianity over something that Protestants and Catholics agree happens, but simply name as something else?

Sola fide

Good questions—and they lead directly into the second impassible difference between Protestantism and Rome on justification: *the means* of salvation. Is it by faith alone (what the Protestant Reformers called *sola fide*) or by faith plus something else as well? The answer depends upon how one understands the first difference—whether justification is a legal declaration of righteousness or if it also includes the infusion of saving righteousness into the believer.

Interestingly enough, Catholics staunchly believe in salvation by faith. The Council of Trent expressed it like this: "[W]e are therefore said to be justified by faith, because faith is the beginning of human salvation, the foundation and root of all justification, without which it is impossible to please God, and to come into the fellowship of His sons."[22] The *Catechism of the Catholic Church* says it too: "Believing in Jesus Christ and in the One who sent him for our salvation is necessary for obtaining that salvation. 'Since without faith it is impossible to please [God]' and to attain to the fellowship of his sons, therefore without faith no one has ever attained justification, nor will anyone obtain eternal life 'but he who endures to the end.' "[23] And again, according to the *Catechism:* "Faith is necessary for salvation. The Lord Himself affirms: 'He who believes and is baptized will be saved; but he who does not believe will be condemned.' "[24]

Because Rome doesn't deny the necessity of faith for salvation, it could in good conscience sign statements such as this (found in *The Joint Declaration on the Doctrine of Justification)*: "We confess together that sinners are justified by faith in the saving action of God in Christ."[25]

Salvation by faith is not, nor has ever been, a problem for Rome; salvation by *faith alone,* however—that's another matter entirely. Faith, Rome says, is a *necessary* condition for salvation—it just isn't a *sufficient* one. That is a crucial distinction. It's like saying that, according to the U. S. Constitution, a person must be born in the United States in order to be president. Being born in the United States is, then, a *necessary* condition for one to be president, just as faith is a necessary for one to be saved. Yet it's not a *sufficient* condition; to be president a person also needs to be nominated and then elected. In the same way, for Rome, faith isn't a sufficient condition for salvation; a person needs infused righteousness as well. Justification, instead of being a legal act, becomes a continuous process within a person and, as such, can never be by faith alone. The moment justification is deemed to be intrinsic, something happening within a subjective being, the paradigm shifts.

This point, made in chapter 4, bears repeating: "If this saving righteousness were in them, then, however subtly, salvation would still have to be by works, by something that these people do because of a righteousness manifested in them that changes them and what they do, a righteousness that expresses itself in good works. How can someone have an intrinsic, personal righteousness working within them that does not change them? They can't, which means that this righteousness, ultimately, is of their own good works, and that isn't 'the righteousness of God' that Paul talks about, the righteousness that gives us a perfect standing before God."

Once justification becomes something that happens in us (the foundation of Roman Catholic soteriology), then salvation is works-orientated. It has to be. For Rome, justification includes sanctification and "inner renewal"; and what is sanctification and inner renewal if not manifested as deeds, works, acts?

"The grace of the Holy Spirit," says the *Catechism,* "has the power to justify us, that is, to cleanse us from our sins"[26]—and to be cleansed from sin involves works. How can the concept of being cleansed from sin be separated from the concept of works? It can't. When we are renewed, when we are cleansed from sin, when we are sanctified, we do or don't do certain things—and the doing or the not doing of these things is manifested as works (Not stealing is still doing something; it is the act of not-stealing).

Again, to quote chapter 4: "To argue that it's not our works, but God's works in us, is the type of casuistry scribbled into these bogus documents of unity between Protestants and Catholics in order to proclaim a theological unity that exists only in the synaptic clefts of their subjective imaginations, and not in objective reality. God doesn't force Himself upon us or into us. He doesn't make us do good works. If some folks do good works and some don't, it's only because some have made a choice to allow God to work in them in order that they can do these works, and some have made a choice not to allow Him. If God, working in Mother Teresa, used her to feed orphans, it's still Mother Teresa feeding orphans, and all the metaphysical, mystical, and theological sophistry to the contrary can't change that fact. It's something in her, something intrinsic to who she is, that results in something that *she* does, something that results in *her* works—and if these works, in any way, make her righteous before God, then she's saved, not by faith alone, but also by works. The claim that it is God's works in us, and not our own, only pushes the argument one step backward; it doesn't change the fundamental issue, which is that if salvation is by anything other than a righteousness outside of us, then it is, of necessity, by our works, whether their origin is or is not in God."

According to the Council of Trent: "If anyone says that man can be justified before God by his own works, whether done by his own natural powers or through the teaching of the law, *without divine grace through Jesus,* let him be anathema."[27] The phrase "without divine grace" reveals everything. Rome condemns justification by works that are not grace-motivated or grace-inspired; it does not condemn salvation by works in general. It's like saying, "We condemn all acts of terrorism not motivated by a sincere desire to liberate oppressed people." Some acts of terrorism, but not all, are condemned. Rome qualifies, places parameters around, and sets limits on the works that cannot save us—a vast difference from the Protestant position that rejects *any* works as meritorious or saving (apart from Christ's finished work two thousand years ago). The quote above from the Council of Trent could, fairly, be restated to say that we are justified through works of the law *provided it's God's grace that enables us to do those works.*

That's what the new catechism says, because that's Rome's position: "The merit of man before God in the Christian life arises from the fact that God *has freely chosen to associate man with the work of his grace*. The fatherly action of God is first on his own initiative, and then follows man's free acting through his collaboration, so that the merit of good works is to be attributed in the first place to the grace of God, then to the faithful."[28] (underline supplied) The italics in that statement are Rome's and shouldn't be overlooked, because Rome's idea that God associates man "with His work of grace" leads to a theology of human merit, of human works.

Although grace-inspired and grace-motivated, the merit of good works—attributed first to "the grace of God"—is then attributed to the "faithful." What can that mean other than that the faithful are capable, through God's grace, of meritorious works? Though Scripture does use the term "grace" in ways that include God working in us, Rome melds the grace that saves us with that grace that sanctifies us until "the merit of good works" belongs not just to Christ but also *"to the faithful"*—whose good works, then, grant them merit before God.

"Moved by the Holy Spirit," says the *Catechism, "we can merit for ourselves* and for others all the graces *needed to attain eternal life"* (italics supplied).[29]

We can merit the graces needed for eternal life? "Merit" is defined in *Webster* as "reward or punishment due . . . the qualities or actions that constitute the basis of one's deserts . . . a praiseworthy quality . . . character or conduct deserving reward, honor, or esteem." Merit, then, by definition is the opposite of grace. Merit (according to the dictionary) is what you do, what you're due, what you earn, what you deserve. In contrast, saving grace is what is freely given to the undeserving, to those who of themselves have no merit and who by their nature are incapable of ever getting it. The moment Rome states that we can "merit for ourselves and for others the graces needed to obtain eternal life," she squarely, and unambiguously, shows that she rejects justification by faith alone because, for Rome, justification includes human merit, a position she has held ever since the Reformation, a position in blatant contradistinction to Protestantism and Luther.

"Luther's doctrine of justification," wrote Johann Heinz, "climaxes in the sole agency of God, denying categorically any human cooperation to attain salvation and, thereby, any claim to merit. Catholic dogma, to the contrary—as it was defined at the Council of Trent—requires this cooperation explicitly, both in preparation for justification and in the justification event itself, which is understood as a sanctification-act and a growing sanctification-process, in which faith works together with good works. From the intertwining of divine grace and human cooperation, 'true' and 'personal merits' develop for the believer, through which he can earn increase in grace, eternal life, and the increase of glory."[30] Rome's view, then, clearly opposes justification by faith alone. In fact, the Council of Trent specifically condemned *sola fide,* the position that Protestants maintain is the foundation of the gospel.

"If anyone says that men are justified either by the sole imputation of the justice [righteousness] of Christ or by the sole remission of sins, to the exclusion of the grace and the charity which is poured forth in their hearts by the Holy Ghost, and remains in them, or also that the grace by which we are justified is only the good will of God, let him be anathema."[31]

"If anyone says that justifying grace is nothing else than confidence [faith] in divine mercy, which remits sins for Christ's sake, or that it is this confidence [faith] alone that justifies us, let him be anathema."[32]

If, however, Protestants are correct in their understanding of the gospel, and if "justifying grace" is, in fact, nothing else than faith "in divine mercy," which does, indeed, remit sin "for Christ's sake," and if this faith alone is, truly, what "justifies us," then Rome has cursed the gospel—a slight historical and theological technicality that the Protestant movers and shakers of this new-found unity have, apparently, overlooked.

Extra ecclesiam nulla salus

So far, according to "the finest standards" of Roman Catholicism regarding the question *How are we saved?,* two points stand out: first, justification includes the imparting of divine grace into the life of the Christian; second, though faith is necessary for this justification, it is not sufficient—more is needed, and what is needed is the infusion of righteousness into the Christian so that not only is the Christian declared righteous, but in fact *becomes* righteous. Directly related to these first two "standards" is a third: the role of the church in regard to the question: *How are we saved?*

Here, again, the *Catechism of the Catholic Church,* speaking as Roman Catholics to Roman Catholics, expresses itself with rigid precision.

"The power to 'bind and loose' connotes the authority to absolve sins . . . Jesus entrusted this authority to the Church through the ministry of the apostles."[33]

"As a sacrament, the Church is Christ's instrument. 'She is taken up by him also as the instrument for the salvation of all,' 'the universal sacrament of salvation . . . .' "[34]

"It is in the Church that 'the fullness of the means of salvation' has been deposited."[35]

"Basing itself on Scripture and Tradition, the Council teaches that the Church, a pilgrim now on earth, is necessary for salvation."[36]

"The Church is catholic; she proclaims the fullness of the faith.

She bears in herself and administers the totality of the means of salvation."[37]

"There is no offense, however serious, that the Church cannot forgive."[38]

"Were there no forgiveness of sins in the Church, there would be no hope of life to come or eternal liberation. Let us thank God who has given his Church such a gift."[39]

"By Christ's will, the Church possesses the power to forgive the sins of the baptized. . . ."[40]

"Through the liturgy, Christ, our redeemer and high priest, continues the work of our redemption in, with, and through His Church."[41]

"Baptism is birth into the new life in Christ. In accordance with the Lord's will, it is necessary for salvation, as is the Church herself, which we enter by Baptism."[42]

"We also call these spiritual goods of the communion of saints the *Church's treasury,* 'which is not the sum total of the material goods which have been accumulated during the course of the centuries. On the contrary "the treasury of the church" is the infinite value, which can never be exhausted, which Christ's merits have before God. . . . This treasury includes as well the prayers and good works of the Blessed Virgin Mary. These are truly immense, unfathomable, and even pristine in their value before God. In the treasury, too, are the prayers and good works of all the saints, all those who have followed in the footsteps of Christ the Lord and by his grace have made their lives holy and carried out the mission the Father entrusted to them. In this way they attained their own salvation and at the same time cooperated in saving their brothers in the unity of the Mystical Body."[43]

"An indulgence is obtained through the Church, who, by virtue of the power of binding and loosing granted her by Christ Jesus, intervenes in favor of individual Christians and opens for them the treasury of the merits of Christ and the saints to obtain from the Father of mercies the remission of the temporal punishments due for their sins."[44]

For these concepts, kings and queens have been dethroned, nations have collapsed, and armies have been raised and ravaged. Here, with these statements, *The Catechism of the Catholic Church* exposes why Rome can never accept *sola fide* (what Protestants understand as the essence of the gospel), why Protestants for long centuries saw Rome as the antichrist (that which is "in place of Christ"), and why Protestants viewed in the papacy, symbolized by its leader—(just as, for instance, Nebuchadnezzar symbolized Babylon in Daniel 2:28)—a perfect fulfillment of Paul's warning in Thessalonians about the falling away and the man of sin: "Let no man deceive you by any means: for that day shall not come, except there come a falling away first, and that man of sin be revealed, the son of perdition; *Who opposeth and exalteth himself above all that is called God, or that is worshipped; so that he as God sitteth in the temple of God, shewing himself that he is God"* (2 Thessalonians 2:3, 4, italics supplied).

For Paul, the man of sin (symbolizing a system) takes the prerogative, rank, and role that belongs only to God. In this context, some quotations from *The Catechism of the Catholic Church* may serve to enlighten crucial historical and ecclesiastical issues:

For instance, the *Catechism* says, "It is in the Church that the 'the fullness of the means of salvation' has been deposited."[45] Does the "fullness of salvation" exist in a church, *any church?* Or does it exist only in God (unless, of course, "the Church" is now "in the place of" God)?

"Basing itself on Scripture and Tradition, the Council teaches that the Church, a pilgrim now on earth, is necessary for salvation."[46] Is the church necessary for salvation, or is God alone necessary (unless, of course, "the Church" is in the place of God)?

"The Church is catholic: she proclaims the fullness of the faith. She bears in herself and administers the totality of the means of salvation."[47] *The church* bears in itself the "totality and means of salvation"? Isn't that God's role alone (unless, of course, "the Church" is in the place of God)?

If, in many of these catechismal spasms, one substitutes the word *God* or *Christ* for references to "the Church," the theology would be kosher. "There is no offense, however serious, that the Church cannot forgive"[48] would then read "There is no offense, however serious, that God [or Christ] cannot forgive." "Were there no forgiveness of sins in the Church, there would be no hope of life to come or eternal liberation"[49] would then read "Were there no forgiveness of sins in God [or Christ] there would be no hope of life to come or eternal liberation."

Rome's argument that its saving authority comes only through the power and merit of God, who has granted these prerogatives to "the Church," is as bogus as the argument that the grace that creates the "inner renewal" requisite for justification comes only from God and, as such, isn't human works. Just as it's still the works *the person himself does* that justifies that person, so it's still through what the *church itself grants to the believer* that salvation comes to the believer. It's like a man who impregnates a woman and blames God, the Life-Giver, because God is the One from whom he received the means and the ability to cause the pregnancy! It would be bad enough if works alone were needed for salvation, or if the church alone were needed for salvation, but in Roman theology it's both—works mediated through the church are needed for salvation. In essence, "the Church" has commandeered the prerogatives that belong only to the life, death, and High Priestly ministry of Christ. If this isn't antichrist, nothing is.

Here's "the mystery of iniquity," the foundation of all that's Roman in Christianity. It's one thing to assert that justification can't be by faith alone, that it can't be "an alien righteousness," that remains outside of us, but must inhere within us as well (even within Adventism, some believe that). But Rome takes a phenomenal leap further. According to its theology, justification is not only something that happens in you by grace, but you need "the Church"—in which resides "the fullness of salvation," the power "to forgive the sins of the baptized," and "the totality of the means of salvation"—in order to mediate and dispense that justification.

Imagine if the Seventh-day Adventist Church taught that we are saved only through the grace of Christ, but that sinners need the Church, that is, the Seventh-day Adventist Church, to administer and dispense that grace. Suppose our theology taught that no matter what Christ's merits and righteousness, they don't become efficacious for us, as individual believers, unless these merits and this righteousness are mediated to us through the institution of the Adventist Church itself. Suppose Adventists taught that not only must a person join the Adventist Church to have salvation (or at least the "fullness of the means of salvation"[50]), but that he must also partake of the Church's rituals and services in order to receive that salvation. Imagine if the Seventh-day Adventist Church said that Christ's merits were stored up in the Church (that is, the Adventist Church), and that the Church—by the authority granted to it by God—controlled their distribution, and that sinners needed to go through the Adventist Church itself in order to obtain these merits. Imagine if the Adventist Church said that persons needed to visit certain places—Elmshaven, Battle Creek, Loma Linda, the Miller farm—or pay money to the General Conference or the local conference, in order for these merits to be bestowed upon them for salvation. Even the most screwball Adventist, who thinks a person has to be an Adventist to be saved (never an official SDA position), doesn't believe that the Church, as an institution, functions as the vehicle by which Christ's grace and Christ's merits are made efficacious to human beings. We believe, instead, that all that Christ has done for us comes to us by faith—faith alone—without it being mediated through the Church or through its sacraments and priesthood (imagine if you needed an Adventist minister to mediate to you God's forgiveness!).

Yet this is basically what Roman Catholicism teaches about salvation and about herself as an institution. Even if Rome has obfuscated on this moribund position enough to keep her ecumenical endeavors alive, she still formally adheres to the notion of *extra ecclesiam nulla salus,* which means "outside the Church there is no salvation."[51] (After all, if salvation is mediated only through the church, what other position could it logically hold?) Whatever the linguistic footwork, the *Catechism* proves that this idea of salvation being mediated through "the Church" is by far one of the "finest standards" of Rome's faith. In many ways, it is *the* finest standard.

Sacrum negotium

In some ways, the above words weren't meant to be critical of Rome (in other ways, of course, *vehemently* so). Rome, after all, is simply interpreting Scripture according to tradition—and interpreting Scripture according to tradition is a premise upon which Rome is built. To be fair, it's a premise that has some logical basis (more proof that logic doesn't guarantee truth). The issue, here, isn't the validity of Rome's soteriology (our premise, in fact, is that it is not valid). The issue, instead, is *How can any Protestant, particularly a conservative who takes the gospel seriously, claim any unity with Rome on the gospel, of all things?*

After the Lutheran-Catholic accord was signed, *the New York Times* wrote: "In a decision intended to resolve an issue that split the Western Christians nearly 500 years ago, the Vatican said Thursday that it would sign a declaration with most of the world's Lutherans affirming that Roman Catholics and Lutherans share a basic understanding of how human beings receive God's forgiveness and salvation."[52]

A shared understanding of "how human beings receive God's forgiveness and salvation"? Is this quantum or classical physics? Anyone who can read at a fourth-grade level or add two plus two should be able to see that Protestants (particularly Lutherans) and Roman Catholics no more have a shared "understanding of how humans receive God's forgiveness and salvation" than Iraqis and Israelis share a common understanding of the sovereignty of Jerusalem. Apart from sharing some familiar terms ("grace," "faith," "the cross," "justification," "regeneration," "salvation," "redemption"), the two understandings of how we receive forgiveness and salvation are as different as midnight and noon at the equator.

What, for instance, do Protestants see when they look at Rome's sacramental system, which includes things "necessary for salvation"[53]—things such as penance, in which the sinner must "do something more to make amends for the sin; he must 'make satisfaction for' or 'expiate' his sins."[54] Or, even worse (and directly tied to penance)—what do they see when they look at the practice of indulgences, something that mocks "the finest standards" of the Protestant faith?

In Catholic theology, when sin is "forgiven," a person must deal with what Rome calls "the temporal punishment"[55] of that sin. This means that the person still faces punishment even if that sin is already "forgiven." An indulgence, however, can spare the sinner the punishment. Says *The Catechism of the Catholic Church:* "An indulgence is a remission before God of the temporal punishment due to sins whose guilt has already been forgiven, which the faithful Christian who is duly disposed gains under certain prescribed conditions through *the action of the Church which, as the minister of redemption, dispenses and applies with authority the treasury of the satisfaction of Christ and the saints"* (italics supplied).[56]

The last line is dispositive. Rome claims to possess "the Church's treasury," which contains all of "Christ's merits,"[57] the merits of "the prayers and good works of the Blessed Virgin Mary,"[58] and the merits of "the prayers and good works of all the saints."[59] Through these merits, applied to the sinner *by the church,* the penitent sinner is offered an out. Indulgences allow one to settle the debt owed by the sin now, as opposed to doing so in purgatory, though (according to Roman theology) indulgences can be obtained for those in purgatory too.

Says the *Catechism:* "An indulgence is obtained through the Church, who, by virtue of the power of binding and loosing granted her by Christ Jesus, intervenes in favor of individual Christians and opens for them the treasury of the merits of Christ and the saints to obtain from the Father of mercies the remission of the temporal punishments due for their sins. . . . Since the faithful departed now being purified [in purgatory] are also members of the same communion of saints, one way we can help them is to obtain indulgences for them, so that the temporal punishment due for their sins may be remitted."[60] It says again: "Through indulgences the faithful can obtain the remission of the temporal punishment resulting from sin for themselves and also for the souls in Purgatory."[61]

In other words, though your sins have already been "forgiven," you still need to do something about the "temporal punishment" for those sins. And what you do is obtain an indulgence, which (according to *The Catholic Encyclopedia*) is "a more complete payment of the debt which the sinner owes to God"[62] (the implication being, of course, that faith in Christ alone isn't enough to pay the debt).

In the 1500s, the practice of selling indulgences spawned the Protestant Reformation as people became disgusted with this *sacrum negotium* ("holy business"). The idea behind the concept of indulgences is that the church possesses the merits of Jesus, Mary, and the saints, and can apply these merits to believers (either while alive or while "expiating their sins in purgatory"[63]), thus granting them "remission of the temporal punishment" of their sins. However much this idea might seem like some superstitious relic of the Dark Ages, the age of burning witches, of blasphemy trials, and of the Inquisition, this is still official Catholic teaching.

In 1998, the pope released an encyclical *(Incarnationis Mysterium)* announcing that, in honor of the Great Jubilee of the Year 2000, a special "Jubilee Indulgence" will be granted the faithful. Here, according to the Vatican, is how one obtains this indulgence:

"By the present decree, which implements the will of the Holy Father in the Bull of Indiction of the Great Jubilee Year 2000, and by virtue of the faculties granted by the same Supreme Pontiff, the Apostolic Penitentiary defines the discipline to be observed for gaining the Jubilee Indulgence. . . .

"In Rome, if they make a pious pilgrimage to one of the Patriarchal Basilicas, namely, the Basilica of Saint Peter in the Vatican, the Archbasilica of the Most Holy Saviour at the Lateran, the Basilica of Saint Mary Major and the Basilica of Saint Paul on the Ostian Way, and there take part devoutly in Holy Mass or another liturgical celebration such as Lauds or Vespers, or some pious exercise (e.g., the Stations of the Cross, the Rosary, the recitation of the *Akathistos* Hymn in honor of the Mother of God); furthermore, if they visit, as a group or individually, one of the four Partriarchal Basilica and there spend some time in Eucharistic adoration and pious meditations, ending with 'Our Father', the profession of faith in any approved form, and prayer to the Blessed Virgin Mary. . . .

"The plenary indulgence of the Jubilee can also be gained through actions which express in a practical and generous way the penitential spirit which is, as it were, the heart of the Jubilee. This would include abstaining at least one whole day from unnecessary consumption (e.g., from smoking or alcohol, or fasting or practicing abstinence according to the general rules of the Church and norms laid down by the Bishops Conferences) and donating an appropriate sum of money to the poor; supporting by a significant contribution works of a religious or social nature (especially for the benefit of abandoned children, young people in trouble, the elderly in need, foreigners in various countries in seeking better living conditions); devoting a suitable portion of personal free time to activities benefiting the community, or other similar forms of personal sacrifice."[64]

What's incredible is not this teaching itself (though, actually, it is), or that anyone could believe it (that is incredible too), but that Protestants—knowing Rome teaches such things as "the recitation of the *Akathistos* Hymn in honor of the Mother of God" can get the believer time off in purgatory—could, nevertheless, claim unity with her especially on the gospel. The truth, of course, is that on three crucial issues regarding the gospel—(1) What is saving grace? (2) Are we saved by faith alone? and (3) Does one need the church for salvation?—Rome and the Protestants have no unity whatsoever.

Indeed, Rome can never accept the gospel unfiltered by (or one should say "undistorted by") tradition. To do so would, in effect, destroy it (at least as it now exists). Once justification by faith alone is accepted, who needs Rome as the one in whom the "fullness of the means of salvation" resides or as "the instrument for the salvation of all"? The doctrine of justification by faith alone makes the Roman Catholic Church the world's largest redundancy. All that it claims to do for the Christian has already been done through Christ on the cross and is being done now through Christ as our High Priest in heaven—without any institution being needed to mediate or dispense what comes to the Christian by faith, and by faith alone.

Thus, there's no doctrine that Rome fears more than *sola fide*. Who needs the priesthood (which, according to the *Catechism,* has "the power to forgive all sins"[65]), or the sacraments (which must be administered only by the church, of which some "are necessary for salvation"[66]), or the liturgy (through which "Christ, our redeemer and high priest, continues the work of our redemption in, with, and through his Church"[67]), or the eucharist (where "the work of our redemption is carried out"[68]) when, according to the Bible (not the *Catechism*) we are "complete in him [Jesus Christ]" (Colossians 2:10), the One in "whom we have redemption through his blood, the forgiveness of sins, according to the riches of his grace" (Ephesians 1:7)? Nothing threatens the Catholic Church more than the justification by faith alone—which is why Rome can never accept it.

It doesn't need to—not really. As the documents *Evangelicals and Catholics Togther: The Christian Mission in the Third Millennium, The Gift of Salvation,* and *The Joint Declaration on the Doctrine of Justification* prove, Rome can continue to teach everything from indulgences to infused righteousness while Protestants—oblivious, uncaring, and blind—reach across the gulf and embrace her as part of the body of Christ. It's not so much what these documents say about salvation (they say very little, really), rather it's *how* they say it that allows Rome, after four hundred years of vilification based on her basic antipathy to the gospel, to now suddenly be feted and heralded as a preacher and promoter of the gospel—without giving up a single antigospel doctrine. Something's radically changed and, as the *Catechism* proves, it is definitely not Rome.

Though the authors and signers of these documents, of course, never meant it this way, the papers are more about the changes in Protestantism than about a sudden discovery of a shared faith. They are more about eschatology than soteriology, more about apostasy than salvation, more about politics than religion. Though purported to be an explanation about the gospel as presented in the New Testament, these documents are really about the three angels' messages of Revelation 14, particularly the message of the second angel, the one warning about the fall of Babylon. Crafted to announce that Catholics and Protestants preach the same gospel, these statements say something else entirely—*Prophecy is fulfilling, the way is being paved for the predicted unity in apostasy between Catholics and Protestants, and that now, more than ever, we have reasons to believe our message.*

That's what these documents say; the next chapter will explore just how they say it.

---

1. McCourt, Frank. *Angela's Ashes* (New York: Scribner) 1996, p. 18.
2. *Canons and Decrees of the Council of Trent.* Canon 1. Sixth Session.
3. *Catechism of the Catholic Church.* No. 1996.
4. CDCT. Sixth Session. Chapter VII.
5. CDCT. Sixth Session. Chapter XVI.
6. CDCT. Canon 11.
7. CDCT. Canon 12.
8. CDCT. Canon 24.
9. CDCT. Canon 30.
10. CDCT. Canon 23.
11. CCC No. 1989.
12. CCC No. 1987.
13. CCC No. 1995.
14. CCC No. 2008.
15. CCC No. 2027.
16. CCC No. 2019.
17. CCC No. 2019.
18. CDCT Canon 24.
19. Martin Chemnitz, *Examination of the Council of Trent.* Part 1. Translator, Fred Kramer (St. Louis: Concordia Publishing House,) 1971, p. 465.
20. Chemnitz, p. 468.
21. Chemnitz, p. 473.
22. *Canons and Decrees of the Council of Trent.* Sixth Session. Chapter VIII.
23. CCC No. 161.
24. CCC No. 183.
25. JDDJ No. 25.
26. CCC No. 1987.
27. *Canons and Decrees of the Council of Trent.* Canon 1. Sixth Session.
28. CCC No. 2008.
29. CCC No. 2027.
30. Johann Heinz, *Justification and Merit* (Berrien Springs, Mich.: Andrews University Press) vol. VIII. 1981. pp. 4, 5.
31. CDCT. Canon 11.
32. CDCT. Canon 12.

33. CCC No. 553.
34. CCC No. 776.
35. CCC No. 824.
36. CCC No. 846.
37. CCC No. 868.
38. CCC No. 982.
39. CCC No. 983.
40. CCC No. 986.
41. CCC No.1069.
42. CCC No. 1277.
43. CCC Nos. 1476, 1477.
44. CCC No. 1478.
45. CCC No. 824.
46. CCC No. 846.
47. CCC No. 868.
48. CCC No. 982.
49. CCC No. 983.
50. CCC No. 816.
51. CCC No. 846.
52. *The New York Times on the Web.* "Vatican Settles a Historic Issue with Lutherans" June 26, 1998.
53. CCC No. 1129.
54. CCC No. 1459.
55. CCC No. 1471.
56. CCC No. 1471.
57. CCC No. 1476.
58. CCC No. 1477.
59. CCC No. 1477.
60. CCC Nos. 1478, 1479.
61. CCC No. 1498.
62. *The Catholic Encyclopedia.* "Indulgences." vol. VII. *Nihil Obstat*, June 1, 1910. (Robert Appleton Company).
63. CCC No. 1475.
64. "Conditions for Gaining the Jubilee Indulgence." Given in Rome, at the Apostolic Penitentiary, on 29 November 1988. William Wakefield Car. Baum, Major Penitentiary.
65. CCC No. 1461.
66. CCC No. 1129.
67. CCC No. 1069.
68. CCC No. 1364.

CHAPTER SIX

Wittgenstein's Revenge

"Once, [wrote novelist David Markson] Turner had himself lashed to the mast of a ship for several hours, during a furious storm, so that he could later paint the storm.

"Obviously, it was not the storm itself that Turner intended to paint. What he intended to paint was a representation of the storm.

"One's language is frequently imprecise in that manner, I have discovered."[1]

One's language is, indeed, frequently imprecise, and not just in "that manner," but in just about every other one as well, an inconvenience for beings whose civilizations, cultures, philosophies, theologies, and entire epistemological structures are founded upon language. One philosophical school even insists (not without some justification) that language itself holds the key to all understanding, because whatever humans understand, they understand filtered through language—from grand high metaphysics to what's on the lunch menu. Language is what exists between us and the world, even between us and our minds. (After all, how do thoughts come other than in words?) Thus, the deepest philosophical questions aren't about what's outside, or even inside, our heads; the deepest questions are about language: *What is it? How is it used? What can it teach us?*

If language is the key to all knowledge, then we have a problem. *What can we use to study language other than language itself?* If all knowledge is based on language, and the only way we can study language is through language, then what can we learn about language, the basis of all knowledge?

Not much.

Using language to study language is like defining a word by using that word within the definition itself; it's an unavoidable tautology. Whatever we say about *language,* we use *language* to say it; whenever we define a *term,* we use other *terms* to define it; whenever we talk about *words,* we use other *words* to talk about them. Because we can never step away from language, and because we eventually deplete the reservoir of words available in our tongue, then the world can be no bigger, no broader, and no more extended than the dictionary. We are, forever, trapped within those flat, black-and-white, typed pages, regardless of whatever else exists beyond them.

Besides all these metaphysical questions, language poses more practical, immediate problems. The most influential philosopher of the twentieth century, Ludwig Wittgenstein, argued that language is nothing but an artificial and social construct that we impose upon reality. To make his point, Wittgenstein employed his famous beetle-in-the-box illustration.[2] Suppose six people—total strangers to each other—are in a room and that each has a box that only he, individually, can look into. Someone then says to them, "Open your box, look inside, and say what you see." Each stranger opens his or her box, looks inside, and shouts, "Beetle!" Because these people are total strangers, this response could happen only because there had already been a socially and artificially constructed notion that this particular insect, with these characteristics, would be called something that when uttered comes out "b-ə-t-l." There's nothing absolute about the word "beetle." In another language, it could have meant "empty" or "Chevrolet" or "poached egg." Other individuals, with other languages—having looked in the box—would have made other gesticulations with their lips, tongue, and teeth in ways that would have sounded nothing like "beetle."

Suppose, however, that a person with a box is the only thinking being in all the cosmos; no one else has ever existed but him. What would he see when looking in his box? There's something there, to be sure—but what? How could be it be a "beetle" if there were no social consensus, no prescribed rule of language, to name it as such? Whatever is in the box doesn't really become anything until named or somehow depicted. That person couldn't even describe its color, or shape, or texture without a language to do so. He would *see* color, shape, and texture, no doubt, but what are they? They have to be named to be identified, and in our world they are named by artificial social constructs.

All of which leads to a dilemma, because something that's constructed only by society (and artificially at that) doesn't lend itself to absolutes. All we have, argued Wittgenstein, are "language games" in which words take on meaning only in specific social contexts. And because these contexts always change, meanings change as well. There's no architectonic meaning to any terms we use, no absolute Platonic form from which all things, concepts, and ideas are derived. Chairs, dogs, beetles, justification by faith—nothing, anywhere in language—has a stable, permanent definition because these words are used in various situations, and each situation gives words, even common words, different meaning. Sometimes the difference in meaning is only slight. At other times it is vastly different, but always (in different contexts) the meaning is different. To say today that "John is gay" means something radically different than to have said "John is gay" fifty years ago, even though the word "gay" is spelled the same, sounds the same, and looks the same today as then.

Wittgenstein's basic point, even if pushed to the extreme (as usual with philosophers), remains simple: words are not absolute. There's an inherent fluidity and fluctuation within them (as contrasted to numbers) that allows for semantic latitude, even to the point where two people can employ the same string of words, in the same order, with the same grammatical structure, but mean entirely different things. Hezbollah terrorists living in Iran say that they want "a just and lasting peace in the Middle East." Orthodox Jewish nationalists living in the West Bank say that they want "a just and lasting peace in the Middle East." The words are the same, the sounds are the same, and the grammar is the same, but the meanings, to be sure, differ radically—because of the social context in which they are spoken.

And it is only out of this labyrinthian ambiguity of language that the recent documents purporting unity between Protestants and Catholics on salvation could have arisen. If humans spoke with the precision of numbers instead of with the fuzziness of words, if they communicated with mathematical formulas as opposed to linguistic utterances, these documents could have never been constructed. However, by exploiting the imprecise cloudiness of language, by abusing the ambidextrousness of syntax, the signers of *Evangelicals and Catholics Together, The Gift of Salvation,* and *The Joint Declaration on the Doctrine of Justification* were able to affix their names to strings of words that—though sounding alike, looking alike, and reading alike—were, in fact, as different in meaning as Christ is from antichrist. How amazing that the children (not the "heirs") of the Protestant Reformers can claim unity in Christ with Rome on the very doctrine that their forefather's used to condemn Rome as antichrist—and they can do so only because words, by nature, are always somewhat hollow, allowing people to stuff whatever meanings they want within them.

Evangelical scholar R. C. Sproul, in a book attacking the document *Evangelicals and Catholics Together* (ECT), revealed just how far these people have abused language in order to sign a paper with claims as ludicrous as if someone were to insist that two plus two equals five. Talking about Charles Colson, one of the influential Protestants involved with ECT, Sproul wrote: "In private conversation Colson indicated that the two sides of the dialogue do not always agree on the meaning of statements in ETC. This is certainly true with respect to the joint affirmation on justification. When, for example, Rome declares that justification is because of Christ, this means something radically different from what it means to historic Evangelicalism."[3]

Colson admitted that "that the two sides of the dialogue do not always agree on the meaning of statements in ECT"—*yet they signed their names on it anyway?* What is a document, any document, other than statements with meanings? That's all there is. Yet Colson admits that they do not always agree on "the meanings of statements." Then why sign? Colson's words are the semantic parallel to saying that, "The general is a great military leader, except that he doesn't know anything about inspiring troops, leading an army, or fighting a war."

In these documents, then, the signers, in pure Wittgensteinian fashion, not only were playing "language games," they were doing so with enough deftness to cheat history, theology, and reality itself.

In his drama, *The Lower Depths,* Russian writer Maxim Gorky had a character say: "[I]t isn't the word that matters, but what's in back of the word."[4] He's right, especially in these documents purporting unity on the topic of justification by faith. It's not the word, or words, that matter (they're essentially vain, hollow, almost meaningless); it's what's in back of them that counts. And, with this concept in mind—looking in back of the words—this chapter examines the three documents *Evangelicals and Catholics Together, The Gift of Salvation,* and *The Joint Declaration on the Doctrine of Justification.* Zeroing in on the parts related to justification, it will show just how linguistically deceitful these documents are and, by so doing, will help reveal the mentality that eventually will turn the warning of the third angel's message into a political and prophetic reality.

Evangelicals and Catholics Together

In March, 1994, after extensive private dialogue, the document *Evangelicals and Catholics Together: The Christian Mission in the Third Millennium* was signed by about forty evangelical and Roman Catholic luminaries in the United States. Basically a manifesto urging Protestants and Catholics to put aside "needless and loveless conflict between ourselves,"[5] it called for both groups to form a united front against the social, moral, and political forces pitted against them and their shared values. Though much can be said about the document (and more will be in the next chapter), and though it was primarily a political statement (as opposed to a theological one), the few sentences regarding justification and grace represent "language games" in the extreme. In fact, they're more like "Doublespeak," the twisting of language for political purposes found in George Orwell's utopian nightmare *1984.* The only difference is that while *1984* was fiction—ECT is real.

"We affirm together," says ECT "that we are justified by grace through faith because of Christ."[6] A few paragraphs later, the same document then talks about the "points of difference in doctrine, worship, practice, and piety that are *frequently thought to divide us"* (italics supplied).[7] The sentence does not read "the points of difference in doctrine, worship, practice, and piety that *do* divide us," but that are *thought* to, the implication being that these difference really aren't, or shouldn't be, divisive. Among those points of difference "thought" to divide these brothers and sisters in Christ are these: "Sacraments and ordinances as symbols of grace or means of grace."[8]

Now, even the semantic legerdemain of ECT can't hide the contradiction between that statement and the one expressing the signers purported unity on justification: "We affirm together that we are justified by grace through faith because of Christ."[9] As we have already seen, Protestants and Catholics agree that a person is "justified by grace," but the other statement shows that they have a different understanding of how one attains grace; therefore, by sheer logical necessity, they must have a different understanding of how a person is justified. If the two groups agree that a person is justified by grace, but have vastly different concepts of how one attains that grace, then the two groups must necessarily have vastly different concepts of how a person is justified. With such a vast, even impassable chasm on the doctrine of grace between evangelicals and Catholics, the claim that justification by grace creates unity between them is rank linguistic perfidy.

For the signers of ECT to claim that both sides believe we are "justified by grace through faith because of Christ" is to utter a phrase so wide, so broad, and so hollow that it can be crammed with treasure and trash, which are able to comfortably exist side by side within the semantic framework of the sentence. The dignitaries at the Council of Trent, which condemned the Reformation teaching on salvation, could have easily affixed their names to the statement saying that we are "justified by grace through faith because of Christ." In fact, they did. "If anyone," wrote the Council, "says that man can be justified before God by his own works, whether done by his own natural powers or through the teaching of the law, without divine grace through Jesus, let him be anathema."[10] Even the Roman Catholics who burned Protestants by the thousands over the gospel most certainly believed that individuals are "justified by grace through faith because of Christ"—proving that the words themselves, without detailed qualification, contain no more meaning than does the spittle dribbling off the chin of a senile old lady in a rocker.

Indeed, the difference between the idea of sacraments and ordinances as *symbols* of grace or *means* of grace show that Catholics and Protestants have a totally different understanding of what it means to be justified by grace. Far from being some minor theological discrepancy between brothers and sisters in the Lord, this distinction cuts to the heart of the question: *How are we saved?* Either we are saved by grace through faith in Christ *alone,* that is, without the need of an intervening body—i.e., a church with its sacramental system, liturgy, ordinances, and priesthood—or we are not. There can be no middle ground, no compromise. Either the grace of God that justifies the sinner comes by faith alone, as Protestants believe, or it's administered to the sinner through the church, as Catholics believe. The difference between these positions is, literally, the difference between Christ and antichrist.

The following statements, all from the *Catechism of the Catholic Church* (in the section titled "The Sacrament of Penance and Reconciliation") show that when Catholics talk about being "justified by grace through faith because of Christ" they mean something altogether different than when Protestants say the same thing. And even though the immediate context of these quotations from the *Catechism* deal with those who are baptized and thus already "justified by faith," they show that it's a justification of a radically different character than Protestants understand the term.

"The forgiveness of sins committed after Baptism is conferred by a particular sacrament called the sacrament of conversion, confession, penance, or reconciliation."[11]

"The sacrament of Penance is a whole consisting of three actions of the penitent and the priest's absolution. The penitent's acts are repentance, confession or disclosure of sins to the priest, and the intention to make reparation and do works of reparation."[12]

"Reading Sacred Scripture, praying the Liturgy of the Hours and the Our Father—every sincere act of worship and devotion revives the Spirit of conversion and repentance within us and contributes to the forgiveness of our sins."[13]

"The Church, who through the bishop and priests forgives sins in the name of Jesus Christ and determines the manner of satisfaction . . . "[14]

"Raised up from sin, the sinner must still recover his full spiritual health by doing something more to make amends for the sin; he must 'make satisfaction for' or 'expiate' his sins. This satisfaction is also called 'penance.' "[15]

Though, at their core, the concepts behind these quotes contradict justification by faith alone as historically understood by Protestants—and presumably by the Protestants who signed ECT—in Catholic theology everything that is done under the "Sacrament of Penance and Reconciliation" must be done *in faith*. No question, too, that the expiation of sin, the satisfaction that the sinner makes for his sins, the sinner's conversion and repentance, "the priest's absolution," "the forgiveness of sin after Baptism," and the sincere acts of worship and devotion that "contribute to the forgiveness of our sins," all arise only from God's *grace* and only *because of Christ* (after all, the *Catechism* does say that, "only God forgives sin").[16]

Thus, the Roman Catholics who signed ECT had no problem with the statement, "We affirm together that we are justified by grace through faith because of Christ."[17] Catholics have always believed that we are justified through faith because of Christ. However, for them, that phrase means something not only different than what it means for Protestants, but also contradictory.

Apparently, then, the view of the signers of ECT must have been, *Why quibble over the nuances of the words? Why argue over the meanings of the words, when we have the one thing in common we need, and that is—the words themselves? Why worry about what's behind the words when all we have to expose to the world are the words? No one has to get behind the text; all we need is the text. Catholics believe "we are justified by grace through faith because of Christ." Protestants believe "we are justified by faith because of Christ." So what else is requisite? Who needs common meanings when common words will suffice?*

Here is the essence of *Evangelicals and Catholics Together*. What the participants signed on to were only words; all they wanted people to look at was the ink on the page, nothing below, beyond, or outside that—and certainly not at meanings. To the degree that no one looked past the sounds, the spelling, and the syntax of the words, the movers-and-shakers of ECT succeeded in their linguistic sleight of hand.

Not everyone, though, was fooled. On the contrary, many people *did* look past the words, the sounds, the syntax, to the meanings themselves. A firestorm unfurled. And rightly so. One doesn't have to interpret reality through the lens of the three angels' messages of Revelation 14 to be appalled at the theological farce of ECT. All one needs is to love the gospel, love and accept justification by faith alone, and realize what the real issue of the Reformation was about in order to see the semantic charade of this bogus document.

In response to the protests, many involved in ECT (which they said incidentally, "is only a beginning"[18]) were forced to create a new statement clarifying the ridiculous ambiguity of the old. Yet in many ways this latter document is worse than the former, simply because it is more subtle, more refined, more sophisticated in its use of words. But if all you have are words, not meanings, then you need to use your words as effectively and wisely as possible, which is exactly what they did.

And the result is called *The Gift of Salvation*.

The Gift of Salvation

Within three years of the appearance of *Evangelical and Catholics Together,* another document similar to ECT (in that it wasn't *per se* an official declaration by a church body) was released in the United States. Unlike ECT, however—which despite all protests to the contrary was basically a political manifesto designed to diminish religious differences between Catholics and Protestants in order to facilitate the growing political unity between them—*The Gift of Salvation* is, at least on the surface, mostly theology, although it's theology with a political end in mind (see next chapter). Known also as ECT II, the statement clarified some of the more controversial points of ECT, particularly regarding justification by faith. More sophisticated, intricate, and detailed than ECT, *The Gift of Salvation* attempted to mute the charges that ECT had glossed over the differences between Catholics and Protestants on the crucial question of justification by faith.

And it worked—but, again, only if one looks at the words, not at the meanings behind the words. This document spent more time on explanations than did ECT (which, in fact, spent none). The problem, however, is that explanations also come only in words, and so if people don't agree on the meanings of the words used in the explanations, then all one has is an agreement on words in the explanations and not on the explanations themselves. And, that's all that this new document is, words that Protestants and Catholics share in common, but not shared meanings. *The Gift of Salvation* simply pushes the argument back a few notches; it doesn't show any theological unity between Protestants and Catholics on justification by faith. It can't, because none exists.

After a well-done explanation of the Fall and its consequences, the document goes into the doctrine of salvation. Below are excerpts, dealing specifically with the major point of contention—justification by faith:

> "Always it is clear that the work of redemption has been accomplished by Christ's atoning sacrifice on the

cross. 'Christ redeemed us from the curse of the law by becoming a curse for us' (Galatians 3:13). . . . Justification is central to the scriptural account of salvation, and its meaning has been much debated between Protestants and Catholics. We agree that justification is not earned by any good works or merits of our own; it is entirely God's gift, conferred through the Father's sheer graciousness, out of the love that he bears us in his Son, who suffered on our behalf and rose from the dead for our justification. Jesus was 'put to death for our trespasses and raised for our justification' (Romans 4:25). In justification, God, on the basis of Christ's righteousness alone, declares us to be no longer his rebellious enemies but his forgiven friends, and by virtue of his declaration it is so.

"The New Testament makes it clear that the gift of justification is received through faith. 'By grace you have been saved through faith; and it is not your own doing, it is the gift of God' (Ephesians 2:8). By faith, which is also the gift of God, we repent of our sins and freely adhere to the gospel, the good news of God's saving work for us in Christ. By our response of faith to Christ, we enter into the blessings promised by the gospel. Faith is not merely intellectual assent, but an act of the whole person involving the mind, the will, and the affections, issuing in a changed life. We understand that what we have we here affirm is in agreement with what the Reformation traditions have meant by justification by faith alone (*sola fide*)."[19]

Then, in the context of sanctification, it says, "In this struggle we are assured that Christ's grace will be sufficient for us enabling us to persevere to the end. When we fail, we can still turn to God in humble repentance and confidently ask for, and receive, his forgiveness."[20]

Toward the end of the document, however, these words cancel out all the previous affirmations:

> While we rejoice in the unity we have discovered and are confident of the fundamental truths about the gift of salvation we have affirmed, we recognize that there are necessarily interrelated questions that require further and urgent exploration. Among such questions are these: the meaning of baptismal regeneration, the Eucharist, and sacramental grace; the historic use of the language of justification as it relates to imputed and transformative righteousness; the normative status of justification in relation to all Christian doctrine; the assertion that while justification is by faith alone, the faith that receives salvation is never alone; diverse understandings of merit, reward, purgatory, and indulgences; Marian devotion and the assistance of the saints in the life of salvation; and the possibility of salvation for those who have not been evangelized.[21]

The Gift of Salvation—however much more refined and polished than its comparatively crude and blunt predecessor—nevertheless faced the same paradox of its predecessor: trying to harmonize the inharmonious. This document, like ECT, contains within itself the seeds of its own destruction; the *meanings* of its own words (not the *words* themselves) refute the essence of the document itself.

The Gift of Salvation—after rhapsodizing about the common view of justification shared by evangelicals and Catholics—then listed some "necessarily interrelated questions that require further and urgent exploration," issues that, at their core, refute the previous claims of a shared understanding of justification. Most any of these "necessarily related" issues—"purgatory," "indulgences," "diverse understanding of merit," "sacramental grace," "the assistance of the saints in the life of salvation," "the historic use of the language of justification as it relates to imputed and transformative righteousness"—prove that the words about a "common faith" are hollow enough to fill with whatever one wants, no matter how contradictory.

Take for instance one of these "necessarily interrelated questions," such as "the assistance of the saints in the life of salvation."

How do the saints assist in the "life of salvation," at least in Catholic thinking? As shown before (but worth repeating), the *Catechism* claims that there is the "Church's treasury," which besides containing Christ's merits and Mary's prayers and good works, also holds "the prayers and good works of all the saints, all those who have followed in the footsteps of Christ the Lord and by His grace have made their lives holy and carried out the mission the Father entrusted to them. *In this way they attained their own salvation and at the same time cooperated in saving their brothers in the unity of the Mystical Body"* (italics supplied).[22]

Without quibbling over details, there is, right away, one problem: the notion that anyone, even saints, could attain "their own salvation" utterly defies the most generic evangelical understanding of justification. That concept, however twisted and turned and spun, contradicts the core of Protestant theology regarding the question: *How are we saved?* Even though Catholics signed on to the statement—"We agree that justification is not earned by any good works or merits of our own; it is entirely God's gift, conferred through the Father's sheer graciousness," a quote that would seem to contradict what their *Catechism* says about the role of the saints in salvation—Catholics understand that statement in a way that allows them logically to accept both it and the *Catechism*. They can do so because in their thinking whatever the saints did to attain "their own salvation," they did only because of the Father's sheer graciousness, never by good works or merits of their own—even if those merits wrought out by the sinner through his good works are, in Catholic thought, an essential part of the justification process.

Now, besides attaining their own salvation, these saints "cooperated in saving their brothers in the unity of the Mystical Body," another concept that is repugnant to the most baseline evangelical theology. These saints were able to cooperate in saving their brothers through indulgences, another of the "necessarily interrelated issues that require further exploration." Indulgences make it possible for sinners to do certain acts, including the payment of money, to help obtain "the remission of the temporal punishments due for their sins."[23]

Again, none of this defies the *words* (as opposed to the meanings) of the document for two reasons. First, according to Catholic theology, indulgences simply remove the punishment for sins that have already been forgiven, so they are not (Catholics argue) directly involved with the process of justification. Second, it isn't the sinner's own works that gets him or her less time in purgatory but the merits of Christ and Mary and the saints, all stored in the "Church's treasury." The sinner just has to do certain things and jump through all sorts of hoops to get those merits applied to himself, that's all.

Thus, with those meanings attached to these words, Catholics could sign a document saying, "We agree that justification is not earned by any good works or merits of our own; it is entirely God's gift, conferred through the Father's sheer graciousness"—and they can do so without having to change a single word because they simply attach different meanings to the words.

Another "necessarily interrelated question" deals with "the historic use of the language of justification as it relates to imputed and transformative righteousness." The phrase, "the historic use of *the language* of justification," is what is crucial in this statement. The key issue of the Reformation (and it remains a key issue today, at least in reality if not in the surreal, quantum world of these statements of unity) regards the nature of justification. Is it only a declaration of righteousness (what is called imputed righteousness) or does it include imparted or "transformative" righteousness, something that happens inside the believer? Here is the core of the difference between evangelicals and Catholics, and all the fancy linguistic footwork and gymnastics can't change that irreconcilable difference.

The issue is not about "the historic use of language," as *The Gift of Salvation* maintains. That is like saying the differences between Israelis and Palestinians isn't over land or the status of Jerusalem but merely over semantics. The problem is not language; the problem is meaning; the problem is theology; the problem is over different understandings of salvation. Protestants and Catholics have a fundamental difference over what justification means and how it is attained, and no matter how much the movers and shakers try to couch the differences as mere semantics—saying in effect "*We agree on meanings, but just use different terms*"—the opposite is true: they share only terms, not meanings.

But doesn't *The Gift of Salvation* include this line: "In justification, God, on the basis of Christ's righteousness alone, declares us to be no longer his rebellious enemies but his forgiven friends, and by virtue of his declaration it is so"? Yes. And didn't Roman Catholics sign on to it? Yes. Doesn't that mean, then, that Rome has accepted the Protestant version of the gospel? No!

As shown earlier, Rome doesn't deny that justification includes people being declared righteous on the basis of "Christ's righteousness alone." On the contrary, its definition of justification talks about the "remission of sins,"[24] which is what happens when we are declared righteous on the basis of Christ alone. But, again, for Rome, justification *includes more than* just this declaration of righteousness. This declaration of righteousness is necessary for justification, it's just not (for Rome) sufficient—an absolutely crucial distinction that *The Gift of Salvation* had to ignore in order to be written.

The Gift of Salvation also includes this line about sanctification: "In this struggle we are assured that Christ's grace will be sufficient for us enabling us to persevere to the end. When we fail, we can still turn to God in humble repentance and confidently ask for, and receive, his forgiveness." Just about any Roman Catholic would agree with just about any Protestant on these words *as words,* but not on the meanings behind them. All agree that Christ's grace is sufficient in enabling believers to persevere to the end, and both agree that if we fail we can humbly turn to God and receive His forgiveness. The difference—and it's a major difference, getting to the heart of the question: *How are we saved?*—deals with the issue of just how it is that one receives grace and forgiveness. Here, the two religions couldn't be further apart.

For Roman Catholics, grace comes through faith, but only through the vehicle of the Church and its sacramental system, liturgy, and priesthood. "Sacraments," says the *Catechism,* "are 'powers that come forth' from the Body of Christ, which is ever-living and life-giving. They are actions of the Holy Spirit at work in His body, the Church."[25] "The sacraments are efficacious signs of grace, instituted by Christ and entrusted to the Church, by which divine life is dispensed to us. . . . They bear fruit in those who receive them with the required dispositions."[26]

Sure, it's grace; sure, it's faith; sure, it's Christ—all the common words that Rome shares with Protestants. In Roman thought, however, all these things come to the believer—those who "receive them with the required dispositions"—only through the vehicle of the Church, in which rests the "fullness of the means of salvation."[27]

And, of course, Catholics agree, too, that "we can still turn to God in humble repentance and confidently ask for, and receive, his forgiveness." They just have a system, in which the sinner needs the Church, the priest, the sacraments of penance, and the Mass—a whole elaborate structure of ordinances and deeds that, ultimately, lead to the forgiveness of sins—a concept repugnant to the Protestant understanding of how one receives forgiveness from God.

Nevertheless, Protestants believe that "if we fail we can humbly turn to God and receive His forgiveness"; Catholics believe that "if we fail we can humbly turn to God and receive His forgiveness"—so why stumble over meanings?

Almost everything *The Gift of Salvation* affirms that Catholics and Protestants share about the doctrine of salvation follows this pattern: common words, different meanings to the words—even when the document claims to give specific meanings to the words themselves, such as here:

> The New Testament makes it clear that the gift of justification is received through faith. 'By grace you have been saved through faith; and it is not your own doing, it is the gift of God' (Ephesians 2:8). By faith, which is also the gift of God, we repent of our sins and freely adhere to the gospel, the good news of God's saving work for us in Christ. By our response of faith to Christ, we enter into the blessings promised by the gospel. Faith is not merely intellec-

> tual assent but an act of the whole person, involving the mind, the will, and the affections, issuing in a changed life. We understand that what we have we here affirm is in agreement with what the Reformation traditions have meant by justification by faith alone (*sola fide*).[28]

The curious part is the last line, stating that the above paragraph is in agreement with the Reformation traditions of justification by faith alone. But how could that be, when the Council of Trent cursed those who believed in justification by faith alone as understood by the "Reformation traditions"? There seems to be a contradiction here. Claiming loyalty to Trent, the Catholic signers of that paragraph affirm a statement of *sola fide,* the concept that Trent cursed. How could they be loyal to Trent and yet affirm what Trent condemned?

It's easy. The Catholics who signed *The Gift of Salvation* simply understood what the Reformers meant by *sola fide* differently from what the Protestants who signed on understood it to mean. There's no question that the Reformers believed in justification by faith alone as expressed in the above paragraph, which they could have signed. Yet the words of the paragraph are written so that one can be a faithful Catholic—believing in indulgences, purgatory, the sacraments, the Church's treasury, penance, the merits of Mary and the saints aiding in salvation, the need of the Church to administer forgiveness and grace—and sign it as well. Even the clerics at Trent who condemned *sola fide* could have signed.

This is a perfect example of how deceptive language can be in the hands of those who need it to be deceptive. Even when they claim to explain what they mean, they do so only with words; thus, they can provide meanings in ways that allow everyone to sign on the dotted line, no matter how differently they understand the words themselves that are used to explain the meanings.

The Joint Declaration on the Doctrine of Justification

The third and, in many ways, most significant document of a similar nature is *The Joint Declaration on the Doctrine of Justifica-*

tion (JDDJ). Unlike ECT I and ECT II, which weren't denominational statements binding upon any church body, JDDJ is an official declaration between Roman Catholics and Lutherans (and, apparently, binding on both). Signed amidst great fanfare and hoopla on October 31, 1999 (Halloween, appropriately enough) by dignitaries from the Vatican and from the Lutheran World Federation (which represents 58 million of the world's 61.5 million Lutherans), JDDJ states that, despite "remaining differences"[29]—Roman Catholics and Lutherans have the same fundamental understanding of justification by faith, the doctrine that spawned the Protestant Reformation.

"The present declaration has this intention," said JDDJ, "namely to show that on the basis of their dialogue the subscribing Lutheran churches and the Roman Catholic Church are now able to articulate a common understanding of justification by God's grace through faith in Christ . . . and that the remaining differences in its explication are no longer the occasion for doctrinal condemnations."[30]

Though hailed as a great ecumenical breakthrough, a momentous step toward healing the long and bitter rift within Western Christendom, and a declaration that the painful division between Protestants and Catholics was merely a semantic misunderstanding, nothing more than a simple difference of emphasis, JDDJ, in fact, symbolizes one of the most profound historical and ecclesiastical (not to mention prophetic) shifts since the Protestant Reformation. Of course, JDDJ, didn't bring about this shift, which has been simmering along ecumenical fault lines for years; the document is simply the latest, and most dramatic, manifestation of it. All the world is, indeed, wondering after the beast, and the *Joint Declaration on the Doctrine of Justification* is proof.

Yet the *Joint Declaration* is also more. First, it's a powerful vindication of the Seventh-day Adventist interpretation regarding the three angels' messages of Revelation 14 (not to mention Ellen White's understanding of those messages as expressed in *The Great Controversy*). Second, it is a linguistic and semantic fraud. What else could it be, making, as it does, the ludicrous claim that Protestants (in this case Lutherans) and Roman Catholics have a common understanding of justification by faith? Have the Lutherans abdicated *sola fide?*

Has Rome renounced itself, disclaimed its *Catechism,* and abandoned its vast and elaborate structure of sacraments, ordinances, rites, liturgy, and mediation? Neither, of course, has done either, which is why JDDJ's claim of doctrinal harmony is another example of Maxim Gorky's warning that words don't matter; it's what behind them that counts.

And what's behind JDDJ is just more semantic doublespeak. Though more sophisticated and detailed than even *The Gift of Salvation* (JDDJ represents *thirty years* of high-level dialogue between Lutheran and Catholic theologians), *The Joint Declaration* is framed in terms that allow both sides to sign on without having to give up anything other than a little linguistic honesty. After all, if Bill Clinton could equivocate on such mundane terms as "is" or "alone" or "sexual relations," why shouldn't theologians have some wiggle room with more spiritual and abstract concepts such as "grace," "faith," or "justification"?

The following are excerpts from JDDJ that the signers claim as grounds of unity between Rome and the Lutherans on the doctrine of justification by faith:

"Justification becomes ours through Christ Jesus, 'whom God put forward as a sacrifice of atonement by his blood, effective through faith' (Rom. 3:25; see 3:21-28). 'For by grace you have been saved through faith, and this is not your own doing, it is the gift of God—not the result of works' (Eph 2:8, 9)."[31]

Of course justification becomes ours "only through Christ," although for Rome that justification includes "sanctification, and the renewal of the inner man"[32]—words that blatantly contradict the most primary and fundamental Protestant understanding of what "justification" means. With that one statement alone, in which the *Catechism* places "inner renewal" under the heading of justification, Rome has expressed itself with enough clarity on what it really means by "justification . . . by faith . . . through grace . . . because of Jesus" so that any claim such as that in JDDJ of a "shared understanding" with Protestants on the doctrine of justification should be seen as the lie that it really is.

Also, the phrase, "justification becomes ours through Christ Jesus," is so broad and so wide that just about anybody claiming the most bland, generic "Christian" faith—from Mormons to the Children of God—could easily fit themselves and their theology within it. No mainline Protestant or Catholic would ever deny that justification becomes ours through Jesus Christ. Even when they were burning each other at the stake over their different views of justification, both the burners and those burned could have claimed that "justification becomes ours through Jesus Christ," which proves that the statement, in this context, is meaningless.

As the New Testament text cited above says, we have been "saved through faith, and this is not your own doing, it is the gift of God—not the result of works," even if (according to Catholic thought) "every sincere act of worship or devotion revives the spirit of conversion within us and contributes to the forgiveness of our sins,"[33] or even if the "sinner must still recover his full spiritual health by doing something more to make amends for his sin; he must 'make satisfaction for' or 'expiate' his sins."[34] These two concepts, lifted from the *Catechism,* spit in the face of all that Protestantism has understood for almost 500 years as "salvation by faith," a theological discrepancy that didn't stop the Lutheran World Federation from signing JDDJ anyway.

One statement, highly touted as a great declaration of unity, reads: "By grace alone, in faith in Christ's saving work and not because of any merit on our part, we are accepted by God, who renews our hearts while equipping and calling us to good works."[35]

Of course, it's only God's grace, and never our merits. It's the merits of Jesus, or the merits of Mary and the saints, which are stored in the "Church's treasury," that help make us acceptable to God after we've sinned, and these merits—never our own—come to the believer only through God's grace, even if (as shown above) you have do certain things to get those merits. Catholics, obviously, have an entirely different understanding of how one receives grace, a different core that defies the Protestant understanding of justification, a point that those Lutherans who signed JDDJ conveniently decided to ignore. They had to.

JDDJ also says that "as sinners our new life in Christ is solely due to the forgiving and renewing mercy that God imparts as a gift that we receive in faith, and never can merit in any way."[36] Again, Rome can sign on the dotted line without having to give up a thing, because no matter what Rome demands that a sinner do in order to be forgiven or renewed—from baptism, which according to Rome is "necessary for salvation,"[37] to partaking of the eucharist, in which the "work of our redemption is carried out"[38] and through which the Father "pours out the graces of salvation on His Body which is the Church,"[39] to embarking on "a pious pilgrimage to one of the Patriarchal Basilicas" in order to be spared some punishment in purgatory for sins that have already been "forgiven"—whatever the benefits, everything that comes to the sinner comes "solely due to the forgiving and renewing mercy of God."

"Through Christ alone," JDDJ declares, "are we justified, when we receive this salvation in faith."[40] Again, Rome has not denied that it's through Christ alone that we are justified, or that salvation comes by faith (just not by "faith alone"). When, for example, Rome teaches that the church "bears in herself and administers the totality of the means of salvation"[41] or that Mary in heaven "did not lay aside this saving office but by her manifold intercession continues to bring us the gifts of eternal salvation,"[42] Rome can still insist that sinners are justified through Christ alone because everything the Church or Mary does is derived only from Christ. For Rome, all that the Church does toward saving souls and all that Mary does in her "saving office" comes to the believer "through Christ alone."

Statement after statement in JDDJ are written in ways that allow both sides to sign without relinquishing beliefs that contradict and defy each other's interpretation of the words they have signed.

"In faith together we hold the conviction that justification is the work of the triune God. The Father sent His Son into the world to save sinners."[43]

"We confess together that all persons depend completely on the saving grace of God for their salvation."[44]

"We confess together that God forgives sins by grace and at the same time frees human beings from sin's enslaving power and imparts the gift of new life in Christ."[45]

"We confess together that sinners are justified by faith in the saving action of God in Christ."[46]

"We confess together that persons are justified by faith in the gospel 'apart from the works of the law.' "[47]

"We confess together that the faithful can rely on the mercy and promises of God."[48]

If expressed before atheists, or before those who didn't know or believe anything about Jesus Christ and the salvation He offers, these statements would be saying something profound, something truly meaningful. But in this context of trying to find common ground between Lutherans and Catholics on the doctrine of justification and, indeed, on the whole question: *How are we saved?*—these statements are vacuous. They might as well have said, "We confess together that God exists," or that "We confess together that God created mankind" and used those confessions (statements that Muslims, Jews, Mormons, or just about any theist could agree to) as the grounds of unity between themselves. As they stand now, these statements answer none of the important questions that debate between Protestants and Catholics, *a priori*, demands. It's as if writers of JDDJ brought in a telescope to study microbes. They couldn't look too closely at what they were doing; otherwise, after thirty more (or even 300 more) years of dialogue, no agreement could have even been signed.

In the entire document there's only one sentence that *seems* to indicate a change on Rome's part. After talking about the works that a Christian does in faith and love after being justified through Christ, the statement says: "But whatever in the justified precedes or follows the free gift of faith is neither the basis of justification nor merits it."[49] This is a fascinating statement, and if taken at face value would seem to contradict two of anathemas at Trent: (1) "If anyone says that the justice [righteousness] received is not preserved and also not increased before God through good works, but that those good works are merely the fruits and signs of justification obtained, but not the cause of its increase, let him be anathema."[50] (2) "If anyone says that the good works of the one justified are in such manner the gifts of God that they are also not the good merits of him justified; or that the one justified by the good works that he performs by the grace of God and the merit of Jesus Christ, whose living member he is, does not truly merit an increase in grace, eternal life, and in case he dies in grace, the attainment of eternal life itself and also an increase in glory, let him be anathema."[51]

Trent says, clearly, that the good works done by a believer are part of what justifies him and increases his justification (whatever that concept means), and that these works are meritorious before God. How, then, does one understand the statement in JDDJ that whatever follows justification is neither the basis of justification nor merits it? The only logical answer would have to rest on the notion that whatever the person does he does only through God's grace and mercy, and thus however meritorious the works in and of themselves, they all stem only from God and thus are never one's own merits. Otherwise, this statement in JDDJ contradicts not only Trent, but the *Catechism* as well (only, however, if one looks too closely at the meanings of the words, not at the words themselves).

JDDJ does admit that there are "remaining differences of language, theological elaboration, and emphasis in the understanding of justification"[52] between Lutherans and Catholics. Differences in language are hardly minor, when all you have is language to express your views. Differences in "theological elaboration" means differences in how they elaborate, theologically, their understanding of justification, which means, basically, that they have different theological understandings of the subject. And differences in emphasis can, indeed, lead to a radically different understanding of theology. A paper issued by the Lutheran Church–Missouri Synod (which did *not* sign JDDJ) critical of the document, expressed it like this: "JDDJ identifies three types of differences that remain: differences of language, of theological elaboration, and of emphasis in the understanding about justification. But here an important questions arises about JDDJ's own claims. How can there be a genuine consensus on basic truth if the language, the elaborations, and the emphases differ?"[53]

There can't be, of course, and there isn't, despite the claim by the document that there is. And, in response to that claim, many voices have cried out, including 200 German theologians who expressed their "weighty objections" because, they said, JDDJ brings the "Lutheran doctrine of justification by faith into question [and] presupposes an ecumenical notion of purpose which is irreconcilable with Reformations criteria."[54]

Perhaps the most interesting, and revealing, statement about JDDJ came from Avery Dulles, a well-known and highly-influential Jesuit scholar in America. Writing about the *Joint Declaration* in a publication that supported JDDJ, Dulles said that on the issue of justification by faith alone, "it is very difficult to make out a consensus since the Lutheran position is based on the assumption that faith is the means whereby we are clothed with the merits of Christ, in whom we believe. Lutherans reject justification as interior renewal because in their view such renewal is always imperfect and presupposes justification. *Here again, no agreement has been reached*" (italics supplied).[55]

What does Dulles mean, "*No agreement has been reached*"? One would think that the whole point of a document titled *Joint Declaration on the Doctrine of Justification* would be to reach an agreement on the doctrine of justification. Yet, according to this Jesuit, there was no agreement on the doctrine of justification, the crucial point of the battle between Catholics and Protestants, the point that started the Reformation, the point that the document (as its title suggests) had supposedly resolved.

What an amazing admission by Dulles, one that affirms the whole premise of this book that these documents—ECT I, ECT II, and JDDJ—are simply farces when it comes to establishing common agreement on the crucial questions surrounding justification and salvation. There was no agreement on these topics because there *can't* be as long as Protestants hold to *sola fide* and as long as Rome remains Rome. Without a capitulation of premises by one side or the other, how could there ever be an agreement between Christ and antichrist on the very doctrine that distinguishes Christ from antichrist?

Despite the hoopla, the pronouncements, and all the fanfare about the Reformation being ended and unity of faith between Rome and Lutherans being rediscovered, JDDJ was nothing but words that functioned as masks, words constructed into an elaborate linguistic façade, which, perhaps, explains why it was signed on Halloween.

Only April Fools would have been better.

---

1. Markson, David. *Wittgenstein's Mistress* (Evanston, Ill., Dalkey Archive Press) 1988, p. 12.

2. Wittgenstein, Ludwig. *Philosophical Investigations* (New York: Macmillan Co.) 1953, p.100.

3. Sproul, R.C. *Faith Alone* (Grand Rapids, Mich.:Baker Books) 1995, p. 37.

4. Gorky, Maxim. *The Lower Depths* (Mineola, N.Y.: Dover Publications,) 2000, p. 58.

5. ECT para. 9.

6. ECT para. 12.

7. ECT para. 22.

8. ECT para. 22.

9. ECT para. 12.

10. *Canons and Decrees of the Council of Trent*. Canon 1. Sixth Session.

11. CCC 1485.

12. CCC 1491.

13. CCC 1437.

14. CCC 1448.

15. CCC 1459.

16. CCC 1441.

17. ECT para. 12.

18. Charles Colson, Richard John Neuhaus, *Evangelicals and Catholics Together: Toward a Common Mission* (Word Publishing: Dallas) 1995, p. xiii.

19. "The Gift of Salvation" Quoted in *First Things*, January 1998, p. 21.

20. "Gift of Salvation" p. 21.

21. "Gift of Salvation" p. 22.

22. CCC 1477.

23. CCC 1478.

24. CCC 2019.

25. CCC 1116.

26. CCC 1131.

27. CCC 824.

28. "The Gift of Salvation" Quoted in *First Things*, January 1998, p. 21.

29. *Joint Declaration on the Doctrine of Justification* (JDDJ). N. 5.

30. Ibid.

31. JDDJ N. 10.

32. CCC 2019.
33. CCC 1437.
34. CCC 1459.
35. JDDJ N. 15.
36. JDDJ N 17.
37. CCC 1257.
38. CCC 1364.
39. CCC 1407.
40. JDDJ N.16.
41. CCC 868.
42. CCC 969.
43. JDDJ N. 15.
44. JDDJ N. 19.
45. JDDJ N. 22.
46. JDDJ N. 25.
47. JDDJ N. 31.
48. JDDJ N. 34.
49. JDDJ N..25.
50. CDCT Canon 24.
51. CDCT Canon 23.
52. JDDJ N. 40.
53. *The Joint Declaration on the Doctrine of Justification in Confessional Lutheran Perspective*. The Lutheran Missouri Synod. Office of the President. 1990, p. 7.
54. *Position Statement of the Theological Instructors in Higher Education to the Planned Signing of the Official Common Statement to the Doctrine of Justification.* Quoted in *Christian News*. November 15, 1999, p. 10.
55. *First Things* "Two Languages of Salvation: The Lutheran-Catholic Joint Declaration." Avery Dulles. December 1999, p. 28.

CHAPTER SEVEN

The Great Contradiction

Physicists have a problem, the kind that any discipline (be it law, mathematics, theology, anthropology, or whatever) hates and fears, and that is—a contradiction. The two pillars of modern physics conflict. Albert Einstein's Theory of General Relativity, which provides a theoretical framework for the universe on the largest of scales (black holes, galaxies, space, etc.) conflicts with Quantum Mechanics, which provides a theoretical framework for the universe on the smallest scale (electrons, quarks, photons, etc.). The fundamental laws of modern physics contradict each other!

"The two theories," wrote physicist Brain Green, "underlying the tremendous progress of physics during the last hundred years—progress that has explained the expansion of the heavens and the fundamental structure of matter—are mutually incompatible."[1]

The problem is this: one theory can't be right without the other being wrong, yet both General Relativity and Quantum Mechanics have been proven correct, over and over again, often with incredible accuracy. Each theory, within its own specific framework, works amazingly well; however, in certain conditions, when combined, the theories yield opposing results, which means that two contradictory laws govern the physical universe—a situation that defies the scientific assumption of an orderly, simple, and elegant creation.

Fortunately, physicists are moving toward a resolution that will, they hope, erase the great contradiction between General Relativity and Quantum Mechanics. It's called String Theory (also known as Superstring Theory), and it teaches that the basic material of the universe isn't tiny point-particles such as atoms, electrons, protons, and neutrons after all. Instead, according to String Theory, the basic matter of the universe is strings that oscillate in ten-dimensions, and these various oscillations appear to us as matter and energy. The only reason we have believed point-particles to be the basic material of the universe is that our instruments (and mathematics) have been too crude to get us to the level of strings. We would need a particle accelerator a million billion times more powerful than any so far constructed in order to be able to break down a particle to a string, which are estimated to be a billion billion billion times *smaller than a proton!* These strings, however small and elusive, might nevertheless resolve the great contradiction between Quantum Mechanics and Einstein's Theory of General Relativity.

"This is where superstrings enter the picture," wrote string theorist Michio Kaku, "for they may solve the problem of how to embrace these two great theories. In fact, both halves—quantum mechanics and relativity—are *necessary* to make the superstring theory work."[2]

Catholics and Protestants seeking unity on the doctrine of justification face a similar problem, that of a contradiction. Unlike physicists, however, whose contradiction is of a physical nature dealing with phenomena or appearances (thus always having at least the *potential* to be resolved), the contradiction that Catholics and Protestants face is qualitatively different. It is a contradiction *in logic* itself, which means that, no matter how far back they go, even paring their arguments down (figuratively speaking) to a "billion billion billion times smaller than the width of a proton"—there are no "strings" at the end of their endeavor that could, potentially, solve their dilemma.

By its nature it is insoluable."The most indisputable of all beliefs," wrote Aristotle, "is that contradictory statements are not at the same time true,"[3] a point lost on those Protestants seeking unity with Rome on the one specific point that divides them.

Protestants reject the idea that justification includes "sanctification, and the renewal of the inner man"; Catholics say that justification does include "sanctification, and the renewal of the inner man." The contradiction couldn't be simpler, and it leads to an even simpler question, one which—no matter how politically incorrect, offensive, and utterly contrary to the present spirit of nonjudgmental, inclusiveness—must be asked anyway: How does one unify Christ with antichrist on the very doctrine that makes antichrist antichrist?

If these Protestants weren't in such historical and theological darkness, the *Catechism of the Catholic Church* would give them everything needed to understand the organization they are embracing—for in the *Catechism* antichrist is unmistakably revealed. All that Christ had done for us, or is doing for us now, has been usurped by Rome, which has taken into itself, through its own hierarchical-sacramental system, the prerogatives that belong to Christ and Christ alone. This is the essence of the little horn's activity in Daniel 8—usurpation—and it's expressed in pure black and white in the *Catechism*. All that any Adventist has to do is read it in order to see in those pages what Rome has done to the gospel. If that doesn't affirm the Adventist historicist approach to prophecy and the role of Rome in it, nothing will. Compared to Rome's hijacking of the gospel, its attempted change of God's law from the seventh-day Sabbath to Sunday (see Daniel 7:25) is trivial in comparison.

Nevertheless, some crucial questions still need to be addressed. What's behind this spasm of documents purporting unity with Rome on, of all things, the gospel? What's driving these bogus statements? What are the motives, particularly of the Protestants, that push them to make claims of unity on justification by faith, the one place where it cannot exist? And how should these documents be understood in the context of biblical prophecy?

Questions so involved and complicated don't yield easy answers.

A few points, though, should be considered that will help put these events in perspective, particularly in light of the three angels' messages of Revelation 14.

Solely, totally, and only Rome

No question, one of the major roadblocks to any sort of unity with the Vatican—the almost unanimous Protestant identification of Rome as antichrist—has long since been removed in much of Protestantism (a helpful development in fostering ecumenical dialogue with the Roman Church). This major shift has happened despite the clear, unwavering, and irrefutable testimony of Scripture.

However much the prophecies logically, historically, and precisely point to papal Rome, much of Protestantism has abandoned the historicist approach for variant forms of futurism, which place the antichrist (seen as an individual as opposed to a specific system) off somewhere in the future (Jerry Falwell recently proclaimed that the antichrist was a "Syrian Jew") even though the historicist interpretation is the method that the texts themselves demand.

In the book of Daniel, the chronological sequence of Babylon, Media-Persia, Greece, and Rome (of which three are mentioned by name!) prove that the prophecies unveil a successive progression of world *history,* which is why the *historicist* interpretation has long been used, correctly, by Jewish and Christian scholars. It's also the method that, with unmistakable clarity, points to Rome's role in both history and prophecy.

In the statue of Daniel 2, for instance, Babylon (gold), Media-Persia (silver), and Greece (bronze) are all followed by the iron in the legs that extends through the toes to the end of time. What power comes after Greece and, though eventually changing form (the iron mixes with clay in the feet and toes), remains the same power until supernaturally destroyed? It's Rome—solely, totally, and only Rome. Rome rises after Greece and ends only when the world does (even though mixed with clay in the feet and toes, the *iron* goes from Greece all the way to the end, proving that the power after Greece is the last earthly power).

In Daniel 7, after Babylon (a lion), Media-Persia (a bear), and Greece (a leopard), a fourth beast appears, one that comes up after Greece and extends to the end of time, just like the iron in Daniel 2, at which time it is supernaturally destroyed (the little horn power that arises in the head of the fourth beast is still part of the fourth beast). What power comes after Greece and remains (in another form) until the end?

Solely, totally, and only Rome.

In Daniel 8, after Media-Persia and Greece (which are specifically named!), another power arises and remains until destroyed "without hand" (Daniel 8:25). What power comes after Greece and endures until the end?

Again—solely, totally, and only Rome. And because Scripture often depicts pagan and papal Rome as *one power,* and because the pagan phase has long disappeared, papal Rome alone remains—the entity unmistakably depicted, and condemned, in Scripture.

No wonder that for centuries Protestants had been virtually unanimous in their identification of Rome. Many doctrines need to be accepted on faith, but the role of Rome as depicted in Scripture is based upon so much logic, reason, and history that faith, here, is all but redundant. One needs faith, for sure, to believe in the Second Coming and the resurrection of the dead; one doesn't need faith, or at least very much, to believe in the identity of Rome as antichrist—not with such historic and prophetic evidence. Perhaps, because this identification is *so important,* God presented it *so clearly,* which makes the Protestant shift *so dramatic.*

The post-modern notion

A second factor involved in this attempt to paper over the differences between evangelicals and Catholics on justification is the *Zeitgeist,* the spirit of the times. The good folk involved in these documents live in what has been dubbed the post-modern era, an age when notions such as "absolute truth" and "metaphysics" and "reason" are deemed as antiquated and useless as vacuum tubes, eight-track tape players, and "I Like Ike" buttons. Truth, spelled with a capital "T," does not exist; there are only "truths" (spelled with a small "t"), opinions that each community bands together and creates for itself according to its own specific needs. There is no overarching metanarrative from which people or individuals derive a history or sense of identity. Nothing explains everything. No one can find the Archimedean point upon which one can see absolute truth because in the post-modern view that point is a fictional place, like Utopia, Atlantis, and Lilliput. There is no absolute, only individual perspectives heavily influenced by culture, heredity, and upbringing. Objective reality isn't "out there." What is out there, instead, is simply a fluctuating, vacillating montage of emotions, sense stimulations, and perceptions that constantly change in the mind of those experiencing them. We modify our world and our understanding of the world as we subjectively confront it. In the post-modern milieu, one doesn't seek to understand reality—one seeks merely to cope with it. Post-modernism, ultimately, leads to a cold (and potentially dangerous) pragmatism. "Truth" is what "works," nothing more because, given post-modernist presuppositions, what else is there?

Of course, of all people who should be immune to, if not horrified by, the post-modern notion, it's the Christian. Any faith that claims the following verses to be authoritative hardly seems fertile ground for the post-modernist weed to grow:

- "Jesus saith unto him, I am the way, the truth, and the life: no man cometh unto the Father, but by me" (John 14:6).
- "Because strait is the gate, and narrow is the way, which leadeth unto life, and few there be that find it" (Matthew 7:14).
- "Neither is there salvation in any other: for there is none other name under heaven given among men, whereby we must be saved" (Acts 4:12).
- "If any man love not the Lord Jesus Christ, let him be anathema" (1 Corinthians 16:22).
- "But though we, or an angel from heaven, preach any other gospel unto you than that which we have preached unto you, let him be accursed" (Galatians 1:8).

Unfortunately, Christian history shows that there isn't a belief, a dogma, or a trend no matter how silly, anti-Christian, or unbiblical that hasn't infiltrated Christianity or Christian thought to some degree. The inroads evolutionary theory has made into the church proves that no belief is too ridiculous for some Christians to consciously or subconsciously incorporate into their worldview—post-modernism included. Post-modernism has, in fact, created the perfect environment for the kind of semantic fog that ECT I, ECT II, and JDDJ need, even if the documents themselves claim that truth exists.

Here's the irony: ECT I, ECT II, and JDDJ, written supposedly by those who would deny post-modernism on theoretical grounds, actually use it in the documents themselves. Those documents couldn't have been so easily written outside post-modernist parameters, where truth itself becomes something malleable, contingent, and distorted. This is revealed, first, in the slippery use of language that so blurs the edges of words that such terms as "grace," "justification," and "faith" are presented in ways that hide the vast differences in how both groups understand them (post-modernist thinking emphasizes the ambiguity of language).

Second, it's revealed in some of the defenses of these documents, in which truth is turned inside out and backwards in order to achieve a pragmatic purpose. One good example of attacking post-modernism while at the same time using it, is an essay called, "The Common Cultural Task: The Culture War from a Protestant Perspective," written by Charles Colson, one of the instigators of the ECT documents. This essay appeared in a book defending *Evangelicals and Catholics Together*[4]—the same book in which Mark Noll said evangelicals and Catholics should not seek to convert those who live at the "finest standards" of their faith (another statement that makes sense best in a post-modernist environment). Though railing against the post-modernist notion that there is no absolute Truth, no objective reality, Colson then proceeds—in the most brilliant post-modern fashion—to blur the edges of the absolute, to obfuscate the issue of Truth, and to reinvent objective reality, all for the purpose of achieving a pragmatic goal (as will be seen in the next section of this chapter).

In his essay, which seeks to unite Protestants and Catholics, Colson writes that "we must re-center ourselves on the key doctrines of Christianity. This means reappropriating our heritage in the Reformation, as well as our heritage as Christians."[5] Telling Protestants to reappropriate their heritage in the Reformation as a means of uniting with Roman Catholics makes about as much sense as telling Palestinians in the West Bank to remember the Six-Day War as a means of better relations with Israel. Considering that the Reformation was fueled by the belief that Rome was antichrist, Colson telling Protestants to get back to the Reformation as a means of uniting with Rome makes a mockery of history and Christian doctrine. If the Protestants actually did what Colson advises, they'd shun Rome, not embrace her. This kind of statement needs a post-modernist environment to flourish, an environment where the hard edges of reality are hacked off; otherwise Colson would never get away with such historical and linguistic deconstruction.

In the same document, Colson writes: "But Luther also believed that the gospel, the good news of salvation by grace through faith alone made possible by Christ's death and resurrection—had become obscured in the medieval and late-medieval Church. . . . In short, Luther opposed what he deemed to be corruption within the medieval Catholic Church, and, for his pains, he and those who agreed with him were excommunicated."[6]

Here, too, Colson plays the post-modern card, turning the objective into the subjective for pragmatic ends. He doesn't say that the gospel *had been obscured,* or that Luther opposed *the corruption within the medieval church;* instead he says that Luther "believed" the gospel had become obscured and that Luther opposed what "he deemed" to be corruption. Now, the real questions are: "Was the gospel really obscured by the medieval church? Was there real corruption?" Those, however, are modernist, not post-modernist, questions, and Colson doesn't want to be that objective. Instead, he takes these crucial issues and makes them subjective by placing them within a human mind (in this case, Luther's) where truth rests according to post-modernism. It is a brilliant, albeit deceptive, move.

In the context of the growing rapproachment between Protestants and Catholics, Colson also writes: "This new cooperation requires neither evangelicals nor Catholics to compromise their respective doctrinal differences."[7] Of course it doesn't, even when those doctrinal differences contradict each other, even if one side's view cannot be right without the other's being wrong, even if those doctrinal differences have been rooted deep enough in reality to cause a split and keep it apart for almost 500 years. What Colson is really saying is this: *You have your version of truth; we have our version of truth. And no matter that these versions diametrically oppose each other; what matters is that we each have our own truth that we don't have to change.*

It gets even worse. Both evangelicals and Catholics can keep their doctrinal differences, no matter how vast and wide, because they can hide them under a common language: "saved by grace," "through Christ alone we are justified," "we are justified by grace through faith because of Christ," "the gift of salvation." As long as they can agree on this use of words, there's no need, as Colson said, for either side to compromise opposing beliefs about what those words mean.

Colson says, "We have to demonstrate that there is *a* truth before we can pronounce *the* Truth."[8] On the surface, that statement contradicts the post-modernist premise that denies the existence of "*the* Truth." In reality, however, what Colson has done is to make "*the* Truth" so broad, so wide, so all-encompassing (basically it covers any sort of generic profession of faith in Christ) that it can include both the Catholic and Protestant versions, no matter how contradictory.

Colson's problem is this: people can't understand *"the* Truth" unless it is distinguished from *untruth*. Considering that justification by faith alone forms the core of "*the* Truth"—a position that Roman Catholicism has not only denied but condemned—Colson's assertion that somehow Catholics and Protestants are united on "*the* Truth" is the kind of nonsense that exists best in a post-modern milieu. The Protestant version of "*the* Truth" can't be correct unless the Catholic version is wrong and vice versa. Though Colson would never say it, in essence what he means is that the only thing Catholics and Protestants need to do in order to unite is to believe in the existence of "*the* Truth," whatever that might be, as opposed to those who deny its existence—a position as insane as saying that because Palestinians and Israelis agree that Jerusalem exists, that point alone is common ground for unity between them.

"An even more frightening statistic," wrote Colson, "is that 62 percent of Americans who identify themselves as evangelical Christians do not believe in absolute truth."[9] He should be glad they don't. If they did, these documents would have been laughed out of existence. It's precisely because evangelicals are so removed from Scripture, history, and prophecy that ECT I, ECT II, and JDDJ could have been written, promoted, and lauded by those who should have been protesting (isn't that what "Protestant" means?) against the lie that these documents promote.

Colson, of course, isn't the only Protestant twisting reality in order to justify these bogus declarations. In a *Christianity Today* piece defending *The Gift of Salvation,* three well-known evangelicals (Timothy George, Thomas C. Oden, and J. I. Packer) wrote: "In the sixteenth century, Calvin, Bucer and Melanchthon, among others, met with Roman Catholic theologians to discuss the central doctrines of the Reformation. We, with them, stand in that same tradition, committed to the principle of *ecclessia semper refomranda* (the church always reforming), and we believe that both doctrinal Reformation and Christian unity flow from the gracious work of the Holy Spirit."[10]

That sounds so beautiful, so profound—yet it omits one detail: those meetings involving Bucer and Calvin and Rome ended in dismal failure, with no agreement between the Protestants and Catholics precisely because the Protestants weren't willing to compromise with words the way Packer, Oden, and George apparently are. (Responding to those who wanted to meet with Catholics and discuss these issues, Luther once wrote: "Let them go on; we shall not envy the success of their labors: they will be the first who could ever convert the devil and reconcile him to Christ . . . The scepter of the Lord admits of no bending or joining; but must remain straight and unchanged, the rule of faith and practice."[11])

In short, Packer, Oden, and George (along with Colson) live in the post-modern world, and it has provided them the tools and the environment requisite for the defense of these documents and the agenda behind them. In Colson's case in particular, the situation is stark: he blasts post-modernism while employing its principles to achieve a pragmatic end, in this case a political one.

The end of democracy?

The quote that, perhaps, best exposes the real issue behind *Evangelicals and Catholics Together* and *The Gift of Salvation,* the quote that, unquestionably, helps one understand these documents in the context of the United States in prophecy, was written also by Charles Colson: "Only the church collectively can decide at what point a government becomes sufficiently corrupt that a believer must resist it. But, with fear and trembling, I have begun to believe that, however Christians in America gather to reach their consensus, we are fast approaching that point. Most orthodox Christians are likely to find it impossible to support a political regime under which the judiciary—without any legislative license—sanctions abortion, euthanasia, and homosexual marriage. Few believers are likely to pledge their allegiance to a government under which the courts, in the name of 'constitutional rights' they themselves have sole authority to read into the Constitution—can systematically close off any form of political opposition."[12]

It's no coincidence that this essay—part of a symposium (titled "The End of Democracy?") questioning the legitimacy of the United States government—would appear in *First Things,* an influential journal edited by a former-Lutheran-turned-Roman-Catholic-priest, Richard John Neuhaus. This journal was involved in the creation of *Evangelicals and Catholics Together* and *The Gift of Salvation* (it also supported *The Joint Declaration on the Doctrine of Justification*). On the contrary, these documents (particularly ECT I and ECT II) cannot be understood apart from the political extremism revealed in the *First Things* symposium.

The gist of what Colson (and others at the symposium) said was that because of U. S. Supreme Court decisions regarding abortion and gay rights, "orthodox Christians" (by that, of course, Catholics and Protestants are meant) must decide whether they can continue to support the present "regime" (meaning the United States government).

"We do not at present despair of America and advocate open rebellion," Colson wrote. "But we must—slowly, prayerfully, and with great deliberation and serious debate—prepare ourselves for what the future seems likely to bring under a regime in which the courts have usurped the democratic process by their reckless exercise of naked power."[13]

However legitimate their complaints (and they are legitimate to a degree; the "countermajoritarian dilemma" regarding judicial supremacy is an old issue), the crucial point, at least in the context of these documents claiming unity between Catholics and Protestants, is that these people are so extreme that, in the 1990s *they openly question the legitimacy of the U.S. government itself*—a position generally held by the bomb-throwing, anti-Semitic, neo-Nazi kooky fringe of the far-right.

But what does this extreme view (which, in a later issue, they had to revise, at least somewhat, due to the strong reaction against it) have to do with documents such as ECT I and ECT II? Plenty, because the symposium, if nothing else, revealed just how off balance these folks have become—even to the degree that some of them would compromise their religious beliefs in order to achieve their political agenda (the irony here shouldn't be lost; they will compromise the most fundamental aspect of their religion, justification by faith alone, in order to bring about a political change that they believe their religion mandates).

Of course, not every one involved in ECT I or ECT II harbored those extreme views. They didn't need to. The point, rather, is that this kind of latent extremism was requisite to create the environment in which documents of this nature could be created in the first place. Once started, the statements took on a life of their own, sweeping along in their momentum those who might not be sympathetic to Colson's right-wing extravagance or who might not even have had any political motives at all. Nevertheless, ECT I and ECT II are, at their core, nothing but compromises on religion in order to achieve political ends. And, not just a compromise on religion, but on the gospel itself!

If not for the Christian Right and the political rebirth of evangelicals in the past twenty-five to thirty years, ECT I and ECT II would have never been written. There would have been no need for them. Once, however, the Christian Right—composed primarily of Protestant evangelicals (historically those vehemently opposed to Rome)—started to flex its muscle, only to get belted back harder than it itself could belt, the movement realized that it needed the clout and numbers of politically conservative Roman Catholics if it were to succeed.

The only problem was that for more than 400 years, Protestants—particularly these kind of Protestants—had been bitter enemies of Catholics. And, more than anything else, what kept them apart was their opposite understanding of justification by faith and all that it entails. Thus, whatever hopes for political unity these people harbored, nothing substantial could happen until this, the most divisive of issues, was dealt with.

Voilà! ECT I and ECT II are, among other things, the fruits of those endeavors. What they represent (particularly ECT II) are Catholics and Protestants claiming as a ground of unity the one point that, more than any other, divides them—the nature of justification. Whatever the individual motives of those involved, there's no question that what spurred on these documents, at least at first, was politics, pure and simple. After all, how could Catholics and Protestants claim a common religion as the basis for political unity when they were bitterly at odds with each other on the most basic aspect of that religion?

Documents in which *conservative* evangelicals claim unity on the gospel with Roman Catholics would have been inconceivable even twenty years ago. Yet, for more than a century, Adventists have been saying that Catholics and Protestants in America would unite on common points seeking to gain political power: "When the leading churches of the United States, *uniting upon such points of doctrine as are held by them in common,* shall influence the State to enforce their decrees and to sustain their institutions, then Protestant America will have formed an image of the Roman hierarchy, and the infliction of civil penalties upon dissenters will inevitably result" (italics supplied).[14] Slowly but surely, the fulfillment of that prediction is being hewed and hacked out. What ECT I, ECT II, and JDDJ show, too, is that nothing which stands in the way of this agenda—not even the purity of the gospel itself—will be spared.

These documents go further than the italicized phrase in the above quote, because they have Catholics and Protestants claiming unity on the one specific point that they *don't* have in common—justification by faith. If they can claim unity on this controversial point, how easily could they unite around a point on which they really do agree—Sunday as the Lord's Day?

Though of a different order, JDDJ in many ways is the most important of these statements because it represents a major theological and historical realignment of a large and influential religious body. Though not specifically a "denomination," the Lutheran World Federation (LWF) is nevertheless an alliance consisting of all Lutheran churches except one (the Lutheran Missouri Synod, which denounced the JDDJ). And though, in many ways, JDDJ merely represents another liberal Protestant body (the LWF is definitely liberal) signing another ecumenical document with another church, it's still significant. For *Lutherans* (of all people) to claim unity with Rome on justification by faith (of all issues) proves that a milestone in prophetic history has been reached.

"The agreement," said the *Washington Post*, "is significant beyond the dispute over doctrine it resolves. It has deep implications for future relations among Catholics and Protestants, said theologians and church leaders. Many said that the accord gives added promise to the ideal their denominations champion—of full communion, or merger, between the churches."[15]

No wonder. If Lutherans and Catholics can agree on justification by faith, the doctrine that first caused the Reformation, the doctrine that has divided them more than any other, what's left to keep them apart? Not much.

Though not framed in the same political context of American political conservatism (the Christian Right variety) as ECT I and ECT II, the document JDDJ, signed by leaders of both the Lutherans and the Vatican, lends an important aura of credibility to these other statements. If leaders of the Vatican and the Lutheran World Federation can, with great pomp and ceremony, sign an official accord saying that Lutherans and Catholics agree on justification by faith, then ECT I and ECT II can't be too far off in their similar claims, no matter how goofy.

Amazing affirmations

Protestants in America, seeking political power, create an environment that enables *conservative* evangelicals (not three-martinis-a-day Episcopalians or World-Council-of-Churches pseudo-Marxists) to sign statements which claim that Catholics and Protestants agree on justification by faith! And they do so even though the Roman Catholic Church, in the *Catechism,* shows that its view of justification is the same as it was when it damned the Protestant movement and cursed justification by faith alone. They sign, even though Rome has not changed on a single point regarding justification but continues to teach and promulgate practices that, at their utter core and by their essential nature, defy and deny justification by faith alone as understood by Protestantism for hundreds of years. And these Protestants have done all this while making bold pronouncements about how they cannot compromise truth!

Meanwhile, the largest body of Lutherans in the world signs a document with Rome claiming a common view of justification by faith when, in fact, that common view does not exist. And, even worse, they claim unity on the specific doctrine that caused the Reformation—which means that, if the reason for the division is now moot, why continue the division? No wonder John Paul II, in *Ut Unum Sint* ("That They May Be One") could call for unity among all churches. "What unites us," he wrote (quoting a former Pope) "is much greater than what divides us."[16]

Not doubt that's true, *especially now* that the pesky little issue of *How are we saved?* has been neutered.

These three documents represent some of the most amazing fulfillments of prophecy in the past fifty years. Only the Pharisees among us—like those in John 9 who despite Christ's healing of the boy blind from birth could still declare, "This man is not of God"—could fail to see the significance of the trends contained in these statements. Those among us who are even semi-loyal to Adventist beliefs, should look at these events with wonder, with awe, and with appreciation for the wonderful truths that have been handed us at great cost to others and (so often) at little or no cost to ourselves.

And because of these truths, we know that final events will not be, as in the quantum realm of Schrödinger's Cat, the result of statistical uncertainty or of mere chance. On the contrary, the future is as certain as God's Word, as sure as His promises—ECT I, ECT II and JDDJ being, if nothing else, amazing affirmations of both that Word and those promises.

To be continued . . . .

1.Brian Green. *The Elegant Universe* (New York: Vintage Books) 1999, p. 3.

2.Michio Kaku, *Beyond Einstein* (New York: Anchor Books) 1995, p. 10.

3. Aristotle *Metaphysics* (Princeton: Princeton University Press) 1984, Book IV: 6, p. 1597.

4.Charles Colson, Richard John Neuhaus, eds. *Evangelicals and Catholics Together: Toward a Common Mission* (Dallas: Word Publishing) 1995.

5. Ibid. p. 31.

6. Ibid. p. 25.

7. Ibid. p. 36.

8. Ibid. p. 19.

9. Colson, Neuhaus. p. 18.

10 "An Open Letter About 'The Gift of Salvation' " *Christianity Today*, April 27, 1989, p. 9.

11 Quoted in, James Buchanan. *The Doctrine of Justification* (Grand Rapids, Mich.: Baker Book House) 1977, pp. 137, 138.

12 Charles Colson. "Kingdoms in Conflict." *First Things* November, 1996, p. 37.

13 Ibid. p. 38.

14 *The Great Controversy*. p. 445.

15 "Faiths Heal Ancient Rift Over Faith" *Washington Post*. A. 24 November 1, 1999.

16 *Ut Unun Sint*. p. 20. May 25, 1995.

If you enjoyed this book, you'll enjoy these by the same author:

Day of the Dragon
Clifford Goldstein. This book is both an unsettling and faith-affirming look at how current events have set the stage for America's date with prophetic destiny. From first to last, each word burns with the conviction that the "lamb-like beast" of Revelation 13 is beginning to speak "like a dragon." 0-8163-1148-X. Paperback. US$8.99, Cdn$13.49.

One Nation Under God?
Clifford Goldstein. Does Bible prophecy predict the failure of American democracy near the end of time? Is it already happening in our country? In a book that reaches back into American history and snatches events from today's headlines, Clifford Goldstein warns us that our freedom are more precious—and more precarious—than we think.
0-8163-1308-3. US$10.99, Cdn$16.49.

Like A Fire in My Bones
Clifford Goldstein. The author's most important and passionate messages. The best of what he has written over the last 20 years touches on topics such as end times, religious persecution, the judgment, and more.
0-8163-1580-9. Paperback. US$12.99, Cdn$19.49.